P9-BHY-457

By the same author

*The American Farmer
and the Canadian West*

WESTERN POPULISM
STUDIES IN AN AMBIVALENT CONSERVATISM

Karel D. Bicha

Coronado Press   1976

SBN 87291–085–7

Set in 10 on twelve point Press Roman
and published in the USA by
   Coronado Press
   Box 3232
   Lawrence, Kansas, 66044

FOR
LKB
and in memory of
SJB

CONTENTS

ILLUSTRATIONS

FOREWORD

"The People's Party is a party of law and order. Its mission is to restore, as far as law can affect it, equality of opportunity in the race for life."

> Resolution of the Idaho Populist Convention, August 1, 1894. *Boise Idaho Daily Statesman,* August 3, 1894.

"The people I represent are not anarchists, they are not opposed to the accumulation of wealth, but they are opposed to its unjust distribution; they believe that the accumulation of wealth is the first step in social improvement and that the next thing in importance is its proper distribution, [which] if left free to follow natural laws, would be found in accordance with the skill, industry and economy of those who toil."

> William McKeighan of Nebraska, *Congressional Record,* 52 Cong., 1 Sess., 2436-2437 (March 23, 1892).

"We have no sympathy with socialistic levelers, and we are no believers in equality of intellect or equality of powers. But the government which by special grants or special laws destroys equality of privilege and opportunity is on the certain road to decay."

> *Alliance* (Lincoln, Neb.), June 26, 1889.

"Man lives to acquire — to gain in some direction."
"Liberty first, then opportunity for further gain. This is the Law."

> John R. Rogers, *Life* (1899).

ACKNOWLEDGEMENTS

The research for this volume was conducted primarily in the state historical societies of Kansas, Nebraska, Colorado, Minnesota and Wisconsin. I am indebted to many librarians, curators and archivists who staff these institutions for their unfailing helpfulness and courtesy. I am also grateful to James Davis of the Western History Collection, Denver Public Library, who made available to me the collection of Davis Hanson Waite materials in that repository, and to Thomas Domer, Virginia Zarob, J. Philip Langellier, Gerald Browne and Roger Ziemet for assistance in researching the behavior of the Populist delegations in Congress.

The initial phase of my work was supported by a grant from the Canada Council. Subsequently a Marquette University Faculty Fellowship facilitated completion of other parts of the study. The chapter on Jerry Simpson, which first appeared in 1967 in the *Journal of American History,* is reprinted with permission. Some of the ideas in the first chapter of this book were originally expressed in the January, 1973, issue of *Agricultural History.*

F. Paul Prucha read a portion of the text and offered a number of pertinent criticisms. My wife, Roberta, and Mrs. Eleonor Woodward Sacks typed the manuscript. I am, of course, solely responsible for any errors in the following pages.

Karel D. Bicha

CHAPTER ONE

Western Populism: Postulates and Perspectives

The People's Party, or the Populist movement, one of the significant and crisis-engendered manifestations of political reorientation in the 1890s, has evoked the attention of scholars in a peculiarly spasmodic way. Not more than two decades ago the classic accounts of the phenomenon, Solon J. Buck's *The Agrarian Crusade* (1920) and John D. Hicks' *The Populist Revolt* (1931), provided the standard and generally unquestioned interpretation of the Populist experience. Populists, it was believed, were humane, parochial and unsophisticated advocates of a limited but consequential set of progressive postulates, many of which happened to encase ideas whose time was soon to come. Owing largely to the massive effort of the late Professor Hicks, the role of the Populists in the American reform tradition had been identified, verified, secured and accorded common acceptance.

This complacent attitude toward Populism, of course, ended abruptly in the early 1950s, and scholarly discussion and polemic about the nature and meaning of the movement appeared with some frequency during the subsequent fifteen years. Provoked by the sudden emergence of a potent "radical right" in the United States, a group of America's most distinguished academics undertook to discern the archetypal attitudes which underlay the contemporary ultra-conservative thrust.[1] To varying degrees these attitudes were traced to Populism, and the suddenly beleaguered Populists were depicted as xenophobic, anti-Semitic, reactionary in social and economic attitudes, obsessed with the conviction that their world reflected the efficacious working out of conscious conspiracy, and, in the estimation of one scholar, proto-fascistic.[2] By the early 1960s, when the ideological threat of the previous decade had dissipated, a pronounced reaction against the negative conclusions of the scholarship of the previous decade was detectable. Another group of scholars, concentrating upon more basic sources, endeavored with some success to free the Populists from the complex of phobias which attached to their memory, and, with less success, sought to reestablish the locus of the movement on the leftward side of the ideological spectrum.[3] Hence an

opinion offered in 1957 that Populism was proto-fascistic occasioned a rejoinder in 1965 that "Populism is our conscience, and we cannot face it."[4] Yet,
with the notable exception of a symposium which *Agricultural History*[5] published in 1965, the protagonists of these irreconcilable interpretations avoided
direct confrontation, and scholarly polemic, instead of evolving into dialogue
in conformity with current fashions, merely subsided. By the end of the
1960s "populist" no longer connoted anything in particular, and the term has
appeared in recent political usage to depict public figures with divergent and
hostile political philosophies.[6]

The present study has no polemical intentions. It is intended to advance
the thesis that Populism in the plains and mountain states, the only regions in
America in which Populists acquired and exercised real power, was neither
particularly progressive nor especially reactionary, neither consciously "left-
wing" nor "right-wing," but self-consciously rooted in old, traditional and
conservative values. If it is obligatory to relate the movement to the political
"center," Populism must be placed slightly, but not dramatically, to the
"right." Put succinctly, Populism was an intensified expression of, and a
politicized rededication to, traditional American beliefs in a governmental
apparatus of minimal scope and authority and an economy which operated
according to the postulates of natural economic law and an unconstricted,
unmanaged and competitive marketplace which reflected exchange between
small, independent and uncombined producers and consumers. Populists believed these to be the foundation ideals of the nation, suborned by the plutocrats who ruled the business world and abandoned by the major political parties. Populists thought of themselves as custodians of the nation's historic
values, and they dedicated their efforts, however briefly and inconsistently,
to the revitalization of the traditional ideals. But it is also clear that by the
1890s, when the incongruities and inequities endemic in an industrial society
became clear enough to provoke a crisis of considerable proportions in the
United States, that the ideals of laissez-faire and the negative state represented a distinct conservatism.[7]

That the Populist effort to resuscitate the traditional value system was explicitly repudiated by most Americans was clear enough. It has not been so
clearly recognized, however, that the political upheaval of the 1890s, engendered first by serious cultural issues and subsequently by a serious depression,
was an upheaval in which Populism, essentially regional in its incidence,
played only a secondary role. The fundamental aspects of political change in
the 1890s were the demise of a viable Democratic coalition, a phenomenon
which was basically unaffected by the transition of power in the party from
its Bourbon-businessman faction to the Bryanite-agrarians, and especially the

emergence of a restructured and rejuvenated Republican party, which broke the long political stalemate of the Gilded Age to assume the role of the nation's majority political instrument. In the process of individual and group detachment from old political loyalties, and the disintegration and reconstitution of coalitions of interest groups, the Republicans modified their behavior and image sufficiently to achieve a political synthesis which commended itself to a clear majority of the electorate as the progressive political force in the society. The Populist phenomenon was part, and only part, of this detachment-reattachment process, and it is instructive to note that, in areas where Populists offered an electoral alternative to the major parties, the response of the electorate in the depression-dominated election of 1894, as well as in the crucial contest of 1896, was a repudiation of the self-conscious "reformers" and a resounding expression of confidence in the Republicans. The People's Party, already moribund in many respects, subsequently forged a union with the Democrats which hastened the devolution of both parties. Populist-Democratic "fusion," accomplished primarily in the years 1894-1896, polarized and simplified political choices and stimulated the emergence of a vital and fluid Republican coalition, the predominance of which became clear by 1896.[8]

Populists, for their part, displayed considerable talent in the deployment of liberal and humane rhetoric. But the rhetoric was largely subterfuge, for the behavior of Populists in concrete legislative and administrative situations betrayed the narrow, conservative, interest-politics nature of the movement. Populists were not interested in promoting major social change, nor were they inclined to create *new* institutions with a view toward accommodating the future needs of the society. Their intention was the reduction of the size, scope, influence and expense of government and the restoration of the free market of classical economic theory. This, they reasoned, would guarantee *equity* in the political and economic processes for the interest groups represented by the party. The idea of equity was a constant in Populist analysis.

Assuming that men and movements can be more precisely evaluated by their behavior than by their rhetoric, the conservative essentials of Populism can be illustrated by exploring the dimensions of this rudimentary judgment. Three criteria are fundamental in this regard. The first of these is an assessment of the Populist attitude toward the market mechanism, the functional apparatus through which goods and services are exchanged. The second, which impinges also on the first, is a determination of the Populist conception of the desirable location of political power in the society. And the third, and most consequential, of these criteria, is the Populist view of the legitimate role and responsibility of government for the welfare and security of the citizenry, that is, the Populist attitude toward fiscal policy, public welfare and public services. An evaluation of Populist behavior in each of these areas provides measurable assistance in establishing Populism's place on the ideological spectrum and illustrates the conservative and traditional nature of Populist behavior.

It is asserted here, and argued in the following chapters, that Populists believed in and accepted as normative the ideal of a free, competitive, unconstricted market as theoretically elucidated by the British classical economists and their numerous American disciples. This article of faith cut a broad swath through Populist commentary, especially in the form of lamentations for this betrayed ideal as monopoly, sustained by the policies of the major parties, seemed more and more to dominate the market process. Populists represented small producers, incapable of manipulating the economic order, and they were insistent that their situation should obtain for all producers. The anti-monopoly posture of Populism, of course, is so well known that it need not be elaborated further, but it is also worth noting that Populists opposed all forms of subsidy, by public policy or private manipulation, as contraventions of the natural operation of the market. In numerous statements of the Farmers Alliances, and in the Omaha Platform of 1892, Populism's fundamental testament, this opposition was stated forthrightly: "Resolved, that we oppose any subsidy or national aid to any private corporation for any purpose."[9]

Populists accepted the laissez-faire ideas of classical economics in all of their elementary particulars. They were fond of buttressing their case by the citation of economic authorities, and these authorities were invariably the great classicists. Adam Smith, in particular, was Populism's economist, although there are frequent and approving references in the sparse record bequeathed by Populist leaders to Ricardo, Mill, Say, and even Herbert Spencer.[10] A search of the Populist documents for any acquaintance with the ideas of the new, reformist economic thinkers such as Richard T. Ely, E.R.A. Seligman, John Bates Clark and others trained in or influenced by the German historical school with its significant statist predilections is a fruitless task.

Moreover, the final and summary demand of the People's Party, the unlimited coinage of silver at the historic ratio of 16:1 (to gold) explicitly expressed a laissez-faire monetary axiom. Even a peculiar monetary expedient such as the "sub-treasury," sponsored by the party but never pressed by its leadership, accorded strictly with the classical insistence that money be tied to substances of real value—in this case the security of staple crops stored in government warehouses created for this purpose.[11] Such examples could easily be multiplied, but for present purposes they are not as meaningful as an explanation of the seemingly contradictory elements to classical theory which appeared in the Populist policy statements.

Therefore, it is important to reconcile those aspects of the Populist program which seem to derive from "progressive" or even socialist influences with the traditional, classical economics reality of the movement. These aspects, of course, were the Populist advocacy of a government operated monetary system and the government ownership of railroads and communications. Here the critical realization is the Populist conviction that public policy had accorded an unwarranted and privileged status to the banking and financial community which permitted the constriction and manipulation of the monetary system in contravention of the dictates of natural economic law. Similarly, government bodies had deliberately neglected to recognize the inherently monopolistic character of railroad and communications enterprises and to treat them accordingly. Hence public policy had encouraged the emergence of a set of relationships which resulted in unnatural and uncompetitive determinations of the volume of money, the rate of interest, the level of prices, and transportation rates which prevented true competition in all areas of enterprise in which markets were involved. If the financial and transportation sectors could not be controlled by market forces, then it was necessary to neutralize them by public ownership or control and to remove them from the market altogether.[12] Subsequent services would be rendered at cost, a situation equivalent to the profitless condition of equilibrium in a purely competitive market.

Populists advocated the restoration of an economy of small, independent producers, none of whom could influence the natural working of market forces. A classical market was their fundamental objective, and they believed that market freedom would expand the outlets for, or increase the prices of, their particular products and skills. Precisely how this salutary state of affairs would materialize poses a question to which a definitive answer was never forthcoming, and Populist leaders also neglected to pursue the goal of market freedom with consistency. Apparently the elimination of artificial concentrations of economic power was in itself the efficacious act. In the immediate instance the unlimited coinage of silver, with its obvious inflationary potential, offered the prospect of higher wages and commodity prices. It is also possible that Populists believed that the adoption of a laissez-faire silver policy would facilitate the penetration of the silver standard nations of Latin America and Asia and at the same time yield direct benefits to the mining states of the Rocky Mountain region, one of the strongholds of the movement. Yet the unavoidable question still remains: were Populists interested primarily in higher domestic prices, an expanded domestic market, the penetration of new foreign markets, or some combination of all these elements?

This question does not admit of a definitive answer. If the Populists distinguished between higher prices and wider markets, or between the location of markets, the distinctions were never adequately articulated. The analysis was never carried beyond the axiom that prosperity for small producers was functionally related to a free market. It is quite clear that welfare policies designed to provide a direct redistribution of income and thus to expand the available domestic market were not part of the Populist repertoire, and Populist advocacy of a graduated income tax, though potentially redistributive in its effects, was based upon a rationale partly punitive and partly designed to permit the reduction of other levies. The income tax was never viewed in Populist circles as a measure to finance expanded social services but merely as a form of economic justice.[13]

That Populists were interested primarily in securing new foreign markets to absorb the surplus products of American farms also cannot be demonstrated as the representative position of party leaders. A few prominent Populists, of whom Jerry Simpson of Kansas is the best example, were classical free traders and argued that the elimination of American tariffs would permit an increase in American exports.[14] But there is no reason to suppose that Simpson represented a common Populist position on this question, and, in any event, the tariff was never considered to be a consequential issue by the People's Party. And free trade was never a constituent of the American variant of laissez-faire theory except in academic circles.[15] Hence it does not appear that Populists were concerned with actual or potential foreign retaliation to America's protectionist policies. There remain only the possibilities that Populists defined market freedom as the penetration of silver-bloc nations, a notion which was at least consistent with the demand to restore a bimetallic monetary standard but was nevertheless stated candidly only by William V. Allen of Nebraska and John C. Bell of Colorado, or that they favored opening new markets by aggressive tactics, which correlates well with their enthusiastic (but short-lived) support of the McKinley administration's imperial goals.[16] Free-trader Jerry Simpson was the solitary congressional dissenter from Populism's brief flirtation with the idea of imperium.[17]

The sparseness of evidence on the subject permits only the conclusion that Populists failed to specify the kind of market freedom which would emanate from the restoration of the reality of the classical free market. Free coinage of silver offered the prospect of undifferentiated market expansion. And the other elements in the Populist program—abolition of alien land ownership, government control or ownership of the monetary and transportation systems, and the political devices necessary to insure the direct, popular control of government policy—were all designed to extricate these functions and services from monopolistic domination by groups whose pursuit of exclusive self-interest behind a facade of legal and public policy contrivances thwarted the natural operation of markets.[18] Even minor Populist demands at the level of state government, such as the reform of coal weighing, grain grading and stockyards operations, were designed to reestablish honesty and fairness in business practices and to excise monopoly from the market process.[19] Restoration of the unfettered marketplace of classical theory, which Populists perceived to be one of the beneficent attributes of an older and simpler America, was a primary objective of Populist activity at all levels.

Populist insistence upon the reformation of the political process was underlain by the same conservative attitudes. The political system needed to be freed from domination by the same monopolistic groups whose behavior had devitalized the market process and returned forthwith to the ordinary people. This article of faith explained the Populist belief in such devices as the initiative, referendum and direct primary as well as the hostility to bureaucracy and the concentration of power in Washington. States and localities were regarded as the legitimate instruments of administrative prerogative, and Populists favored a wide dispersal of political power for the same reasons they insisted upon the diffusion and neutralization of economic power. Therefore, at a time when the number of professed adherents to the doctrine was inconsequential, prominent Populist spokesmen revived and articulated the old theory of state sovereignty in a number of crisis situations. If the advocates of state sovereignty appeared only within the context of southern Populism the matter might be dispensed with on grounds of anachronism, but the advocates of the doctrine were northern Populists whose personal backgrounds lay in the Republican party. In fact, state sovereignty concepts were ordinarily utilized by the most "radical" northern Populists as tools to fend off Federal encroachments upon the presumed constitutional authority of the states. Among the most convinced partisans of the state sovereignty philosophy were Populist governors Davis H. Waite of Colorado and Lorenzo D. Lewelling of Kansas.[20]

The most important determinant of Populist conservatism, however, was neither the belief in the classical marketplace ideal nor the commitment to the atomization of political power. It was the Populist conception of the legitimate function of the institution of government itself, especially the role and responsibility of government in such crucial areas as fiscal policy, economic security policy, and the provision of services for the indigent, dispossessed and deviant members of society. If Populists were reputed to be "radicals" on monetary issues, they were also uncompromising fiscal conservatives with a consuming passion for appropriations retrenchment at all levels of government. Reduction of the salaries of public officials, for example, was a staple item of Populism campaigns in Washington, Idaho, Colorado and Nebraska. In itself this was a minor issue, for Populists intended, and sometimes achieved, retrenchment on such a brutal scale that all social services were of necessity curtailed. Thus the Populist attitude toward the dependent and unproductive members of society was one of consummate disdain. Commenting on the problem of "tramps," the indigent unemployed who traversed the western states in search of work during the depressed years of the nineties, John Whitnah Leedy, the second Populist governor of Kansas, flippantly observed: "There are no tramps in Kansas, except those birds of passage who flit by us, grim reminders of the conditions in older communities."[21] These were the social products of other places, and the responsibility of other people. Leedy's view was thoroughly characteristic of Populism.

Moreover, the more militant or "radical" Populists were the most vigorous proponents of cuts in public spending and social services. Populists commonly divided into two principal factions, the "fusionists," who favored cooperation and even coalescence with other political groups, ordinarily the Democrats, and the "middle-of-the-road" faction whose members adamantly spurned coalition efforts until the end of the Populist movement. The latter group comprised the "radical" faction, and within this element were the party's most dedicated fiscal conservatives. On the matter of railroad regulation, an issue of importance to Populists of all shades of opinion, the fusionist bloc uniformly favored regulation by a quasi-judicial board or commission armed with flexible authority over transportation rates. This necessarily involved the creation (or maintenance) of a bureaucratic apparatus, and the commission idea was absolutely unpalatable to the "middle-of-the-road" faction. A commission necessitated bureaucracy and entailed unnecessary cost, and the radical faction therefore favored the cheaper alternative of establishing maximum rates by statute. The conflict between the partisans of these two philosophies of railroad regulation not infrequently vitiated the party's capacity for effective action on this as well as other issues.[22]

The three prominent attributes of Populism explored in this study—the belief in a free market, the revival of state sovereignty doctrine, and the reduction of appropriations and social services—converged remarkably in the thought and advocacy of one major Populist figure, John Rankin Rogers of Washington. Rogers, whose reform career commenced in the later 1880s in Kansas, was an arch-conservative who was unable to accept the reality of an industrialized nation and who considered cities to be "sink holes of civilization" where men lost their perspective and betrayed their values.[23] An unregenerate old Jeffersonian and an ardent pamphleteer, Rogers contributed one distinctive idea to the agrarian insurgency of the 1890s. Convinced that production and distribution were irretrievably dominated by agents of the money power and that rights conferred upon men by a beneficent nature had been substantially diminished, Rogers proposed to reassert man's natural right to the use of the soil. Specifically, his unique proposition called for the grant of a homestead to every family and the exemption of this homestead from taxation or any form of legal encumbrance up to a maximum sum of $2,500. This minimum grant would thus be free from the impact of market forces and excluded from all future considerations of public policy and would exist, therefore, outside of the market matrix. The homestead would afford a measure of security, a guaranteed minimum income to all families, but beyond that Rogers assumed that markets would function freely and normally in all respects. The administrative agency which he proposed to implement the homestead scheme was the state, and he suggested that the state of Washington, which he served as governor from 1897 to 1901, should act as a model for the remainder of the nation. Once the homestead system was operative, Rogers reasoned, governments would be able to dispense with their welfare functions and to reduce their fiscal and public roles to an absolute minimum.[24] It is little wonder that he often cited the writings of Herbert Spencer with approbation. Rogers' homestead proposal contained, in neat juxtaposition, three essential ingredients of Populism: the competitive marketplace, the emphasis upon the states, and the desire to dispense with governmental involvement with and responsibility for the security and welfare of the populace.

If any other recognizable group in America shared the attitudes and convictions common to Populism, the most precise parallels may be found among that body of blue-blooded gentry of Yankee background usually designated as "mugwumps." While this observation may seem peculiar at first, there were numerous and striking attitudinal and ideological elements which served to connect the two groups. Populists, in fact, were a species of regional mugwump. Populists and mugwumps, of course, drew their members from different regions and different social strata, and the two groups differed significantly on the money question and the issue of imperialism in the 1890s. Mugwumps comprised an old elite suddenly shorn of influence, while Populists were normally people who had never exerted particular influence. In spite of these differentials, the similarities between Populists and mugwumps easily overshadowed the dissimilarities.[25]

Both groups professed unqualified belief in the morality and economic efficacy of the classical marketplace, and both detested the new plutocracy for its power to contravene the dictates of the market. Both gave assent to the old ideal that citizens had a fiduciary obligation to render public service without the expectation of direct reward, and both were contemptuous of machine politics and politicians. Both opposed the growing centralization of power in the Federal government. Both drew their leadership from men of old-stock, especially Yankee, background. Both believed that the authority and expense of government were excessive and advocated retrenchment in appropriations and governmental responsibility. Most significantly, however, both Populists and mugwumps affirmed that the established political parties were too corrupt to merit unqualified support especially in view of their inability to conduct the nation's affairs with honesty, economy and businesslike efficiency. Both groups accepted the postulate that a purer and more equitable society had once been characteristic of America. And both mugwumpery and Populism were, by definition, explicit repudiations of the traditional forms of partisanship in public life.

In fact, the Populist-mugwump congruence had a pragmatic, operative dimension in areas where both groups were represented. The state of Wisconsin, which contained a sufficient number of persons of New England ancestry to produce a noticeable group of mugwumps and which also generated a small but active Populist movement, afforded a good example of the two groups functioning in tandem. Throughout the 1890s, and especially in the depressed middle years of the decade, Populists and mugwumps in numerous Wisconsin municipalities made common cause with each other in pursuit of such goals as budget retrenchment, tax reform (i.e. tax reduction), and the curbing of socially irresponsible public utilities enterprises. It is, of course, possible to make too much of the attitudinal coalescence of Populist and mugwump, but it is also clear that they were, at the least, ideological first cousins.[26]

The thesis of Populist conservatism accounts for most of the reality of the movement, but, like any other historical thesis, it contains its share of incongruities and leaves its share of loose ends. In one significant way for example, Populism did point America in a progressive direction. As a new political manifestation Populism was not obliged to carry as much of the residue and cultural baggage of the past as the major parties. As westerners, Populists viewed the exploitative East with hostility and distrust, but they compensated for this polarization by the conscious promotion of rapprochement between North and South, a task made feasible by Populism's non-involvement with the political vestiges of the Civil War period.[27] Nevertheless, the rapprochement efforts were probably motivated more by political than idealistic considerations, for Populism's national prospects were entirely dependent upon the forging of an effective West-South axis. In any event a West-South coalition was necessary to thwart the efforts of eastern monopolies to convert the remainder of the nation into a perpetual economic hinterland. Yet the specific affirmation by some Populist leaders that the bloody-shirt was obsolete was in itself progressive, and such memorable events as the election to

Congress in 1892 of a former Confederate cavalry officer by Kansas Populists could not have occurred in the context of the established parties.[28] In a small way Populists helped to establish a *terminus ad quem* to the shopworn issues of the previous generation.

On the other hand, close scrutiny of the Populist performance in the western states cannot fail to show that Populism was a movement beset with frightful ambivalence and contradiction. Three primary factors render this conclusion inescapable. The first is a realization of the attenuated nature of the involvement of Populist leaders with their own cause, a realization which must of necessity cast some doubt upon the sincerity of their convictions. While many of the Populist leaders had associated themselves with various dissident causes before the 1890s, it was a distinct rarity to find them as active participants in the reform activities of the "progressive" period which followed. The ease with which Populist leaders divested themselves of the cause, and the numerous instances of the explicit cooption of Populists by the forces of the once-hated plutocracy, were stark reminders of the transitory nature of the Populist movement.

But the failure of Populists to persist in their convictions was not as consequential as the frequent and repeated instances of the disinclination of Populist leaders to pursue the party's objectives while engaged in its service. Numerous instances of the disregard of Populism by Populists appear in the following chapters. As a preliminary generalization, however, it can be asserted that if the detailed demands and recommendations of the People's Party's Omaha Platform of 1892 were set beside the record of programmatic espousal which emanated from Populist congressmen in the period 1891-1899 a connection between the two would be difficult to discern.

Thirdly, the philosophic conservatism endemic in the Populist movement itself severely constrained its reform potential, if, indeed, it did not negate it altogether. Like all good conservatives, Populists were inextricably bound to law and to the ideal of legitimacy.[29] Thus they were unable to transcend the limited framework of their own values, particularly the disposition to believe that all social problems were resolvable in a free market context. The market orientation obliged them to treat with reverence the rights of property, contract, and legal possession — no matter how shabby or unnatural the original terms of acquisition. John Rankin Rogers, for example, took extreme pains to lay a solid basis for his free homestead scheme within the matrix of natural rights philosophy, and he elaborated at length the idea that the contemporary structure of wealth and property ownership had been achieved by conscious and willful contravention of natural law. But in spite of his impressive polemic against the monopolists and "centralizers" who had deprived the populace of their natural right to use of the earth, "a crime only inferior in wickedness to the crime of taking away their lives or personal liberties," Rogers had to concede that the rights of present possessors were legitimate and deserving of protection. Thus, his free homestead scheme foundered upon the rocks of contradiction, for no matter how adamantly he affirmed that only an exodus to the soil would counteract the impoverishment of the people, the inevitability of revolution, and an inescapable reversion to barbarism, he also realized that the supply of land available for homesteads, given the contemporary pattern of ownership, was plainly inadequate. Since he was unable to suggest a workable plan for the acquisition of homestead lands, he unwittingly conceded the unfeasibility of the free homestead proposal.[30] Imprisoned by the contradictory postulates of natural rights theory and legitimacy, the utility of Rogers' "guaranteed income" proposal was negligible.

Rogers' problem was Populism's problem. Attainment of Populism's ideals was checkmated by the norms of the movement's philosophy. The aspirations of Populists to free the market, restore the political process to the people, and reduce the scope and responsibility of government conflicted with existing practices, precedents, legal forms, and the majority conception of the public interest, and the activities of the People's Party demonstrated that it was too late in the American experience for Populism. Populists did not, and philosophically could not, transcend the limitations of their own assumptions and values, all of which were rooted in the presumed reality of an older America.

It is not possible to make a place for Populism in the tradition of modern "liberal" or "progressive" reform with its statist assumptions, its affirmation of the direct responsibility of government for the public welfare, and its moderate redistributive philosophy of income and wealth. Populists were nineteenth century men, offended by the corporate and institutional world in which they lived, but irrevocably tied to classical or laissez-faire assumptions. Within that tradition-bound framework they pursued their interests, and the destabilizing attributes of the 1890s gave thrust and focus to their activities. The formidable producer bias and limited intellectual scope of Populism were unmistakable, although the tenuous nature of the commitment of many Populist leaders to the party, and the ambivalent and contradictory way in which they pursued its interests, must mitigate this conclusion to some extent. And the ease with which many party spokesmen passed into the service of the "enemy" demonstrated that it would be erroneous to think of Populists as completely inflexible.[31] Moreover, Populists contributed something to the reshuffling and reallocation of political loyalties which eventuated in the emergence of the Republican party as the nation's majority political vehicle, and they played a minor role in finalizing the normalization of relations between North and South as well as in the improvement of race relations, both in the South and the West.[32]

Yet the true bases of Populism were the restoration of the classical market and the atomized polity, and the diminution of the dimensions and responsibility of government. As true representatives of what Robert H. Wiebe called the "island community," Populists accepted the ideal of small units and a broad dispersal of power as traditional and desirable.[33] By the 1890s, as the crises and dislocations of the decade amply demonstrated, the economic maturation of the United States had converted the "laissez-faire liberalism" of the nineteenth century, premised on the natural law economics of the great classicists from Adam Smith to Alfred Marshall, into a profoundly conservative set of values and assumptions. But Populists normally adhered to the old dogmas and occasionally a lucid statement of their deepest convictions came to the surface. At the 1894 convention of the People's Party of Idaho, for example, the delegates approved this succinct and forthright resolution: "The People's Party is a party of law and order. Its mission is to restore, as far as law can affect it, equality of opportunity in the race for life."[34]

Populism contributed nothing of a positive nature to deal with the recurrent problems of depression, unemployment, and natural disasters, nor did Populists confront the issues of social security and economic welfare in a responsible manner. They obviously believed that these matters lay outside of the scope of direct governmental concern. For these reasons Populism does not merit a place in the tradition of modern "liberal" reform.[35]

In the subsequent chapters the conservative nature of Populism will be explored in detail. The analysis is built around the careers of four of the most prominent western Populists: Jerry Simpson of Kansas, the recognized leader of the party's delegation in the House of Representatives and the only Populist congressman with political longevity sufficient to insure his presence in the House at both the beginning and the end of the movement; William Vincent Allen of Nebraska, who occupied a similar position and fulfilled a similar role in the United States Senate; and the two most prominent Populist governors, Lorenzo Dow Lewelling of Kansas and Davis Hanson Waite of Colorado, who represented the plains state and mountain state variants of Populism in executive capacities.[36] Finally, an assessment of the two significant collective groups of Populists, the state legislators of the seven western states most influenced by the movement and the Populist delegations in the Federal House of Representatives, will be offered as further demonstration of the conservative reality of the western insurgency of the 1890s.

PERSONALITIES

CHAPTER TWO

Jerry Simpson: Populist without Principle

Sockless Jerry Simpson is a name "that sticks to the memory with the powerful adhesion of one of the new plastic glues,"[1] wrote the journalist Gerald W. Johnson in a book inspired by the ideological paranoia of the 1950s. Though scholars have never subjected Simpson's political career and philosophy to close examination, the "Sockless Socrates" of Kansas has consistently received a prominent paragraph in the usual descriptive roster of Populist leaders, and it is a safe assumption that even the most casual student of the American past can establish him in time and place. Perhaps it is true that Simpson, with "the possible exception of Mary Elizabeth Lease," was "the most famous Kansas Populist."[2] A recent student of Kansas Populism has identified most of Simpson's attributes: a Lincolnesque personality, a homespun political style, a quaint expression, and a folk wit.[3] Moreover, Simpson, unlike many of his contemporaries, presumably "remained a Populist from beginning to end ... and died unreconstructed ...,"[4] thus earning a reputation for fidelity to the cause.

Simpson was born in New Brunswick in 1842, worked as a sailor on the Great Lakes for twenty-three years, and finally settled in Kansas in 1878 and shortly thereafter located on a stock farm near Medicine Lodge in Barber County.[5] By 1880, his third-party sympathies had flowered, and he adhered successively (and cumulatively) to the principles of the Greenback party, Henry George, the Union Labor party, the Alliance, and the People's party.[6] In two attempts to win a seat in the Kansas legislature—as an Independent (Greenback) candidate in 1886 and as a Union Labor candidate in 1888—he made no profound impression;[7] but with the unintended assistance of Victor Murdock of the Wichita *Eagle,* author of the specious "sockless" tale, Simpson achieved instantaneous national notoriety in the political pentecost of 1890.

Facing photograph: Jeremiah Simpson, with grateful acknowledgment to The Kansas State Historical Society, Topeka, Kansas.

Simpson represented the spacious Seventh District of Kansas in the Fifty-second, Fifty-third, and Fifty-fifth congresses; he was elected as a People's party candidate with tacit Democratic endorsement in 1890, a Populist with formal Democratic endorsement in 1892, and as a fusionist in 1896. His district, the "Big Seventh," consisted of a substantial block of counties in south-central and southwest Kansas, an area in which the Kansas boom of the 1880s had reached reckless heights and in which the subsequent collapse had produced disastrous results. Mortgage indebtedness, falling prices, and crop failures combined to create a volatile political milieu which Simpson exploited successfully in 1890.[8]

Economic depression facilitated the penetration of the district by the Alliance, and the farm organization provided an appropriate mechanism for the emergence of Jerry Simpson. The Alliance evolved as a significant force in the Big Seventh in 1889, and immediately the members formed a rudimentary political party, securing the allegiance of the older reform and agrarian interest groups—the Union Labor party (a composite of Greenbackers and single-tax advocates),[9] the Knights of Labor, the Grange, the Industrial Union, and the Farmers Mutual Benefit Association.[10] By accretion, the new political entity acquired leadership, adherents, and doctrines. While the doctrinal core of the new movement was the St. Louis Platform of 1889, reflecting the predominance of the Alliance, Alliance views on land, labor, transportation, and monetary policy were supplemented by demands for service pensions, women's suffrage, immigration restriction, and the prohibition of Oriental and contract labor—items culled from the Union Labor platform of 1888.[11] Simpson, himself a product of the growing reform sentiment, wholeheartedly accepted this reform posture with the single exception of pensions for veterans. Attacking this plank at the Alliance convention in July, 1890, he set off a verbal skirmish which resulted in his nomination.[12] Election, amid the revivalistic atmosphere of Kansas in 1890, proved to be less than difficult.

To assess Simpson accurately, given the vicious partisanship of Kansas politics in the period, is a hazardous undertaking. His opponents portrayed him as a boor and an uncouth illiterate, as a monkey or orangutan, as barely human, as a failure who could rise only to the $40-a-month position of marshal of Medicine Lodge, a position which necessitated only moderate skill in handling lost children, stray dogs, and recalcitrant cows.[13] It was undoubtedly true, however, that in order to confuse his opponents Simpson "assumed a crudity to which he was by nature a stranger...."[14] Surely he used the "sockless" epithet as a means of securing publicity, attention, and votes. That the tactic succeeded was obvious enough. William Allen White recalled with relish the occasion of Simpson's renomination in 1892:

In the year of Our Lord, 1892 the opera house at Wichita was crowded with a sweating, snorting, hilarious throng. It was assembled to nominate Jerry Simpson for Congress. It was impatient. Every half-hour someone making a speech seconding a motion to appoint some committee would let out Simpson's name. It was greeted with a thunder of applause—always. A little old pipe-voiced codger in the gallery kept injecting into the proceedings a quavering interrogatory cheep "Hurrah for Jerry!" Then the crowd went into spasms. The word "Jerry" was sort of a holy word.[15]

While Simpson was anathema to respectable Republicans and the beloved "our Jerry" to his supporters, the essential political character of the man is difficult to extract from this outpouring of adulation and abuse. Simpson compounded the difficulty in 1901 by destroying the correspondence of his public career;[16] and his widow, replying to a later query, stated that she had no letters belonging to her husband, "only an old bow tie."[17] Simpson made few formal addresses when in Congress, and his speeches on the campaign trail were, of course, repetitious. Aside from a few letters to newspapers and three brief articles,[18] he left little behind save a sixteen-month run of *Jerry Simpson's Bayonet,* a newspaper which reflected his verbal instructions but rarely his authorship.[19] "Readin' and 'rithmetic wer his," the congressman's widow recalled of the reformer, "but spellin' and writin' wer not."[20]

In consequence of the paucity of extant material, the composite stereotype of Simpson is largely a derivative from the observations of Hamlin Garland and the recollections of White.[21] The standard image is one of a self-educated man with considerable rhetorical talent and more than ordinary comprehension of public issues. "Jerry Simpson," as White noted, "was not a sockless clown. He accepted the portrait which the Republicans made of him as an ignorant fool because it helped him to talk to the crowds that gathered to hear him.... The real Jerry Simpson profited by the fame of his own effigy."[22]

Unfortunately, few of the observations of Simpson's contemporaries offer much insight into his performance as a reform figure; Simpson was rarely what he purported to be. His claim to be a "genuine dirtfarmer," for example, was highly dubious. A favorably impressed New York reporter deduced from Simpson's handshake that "Jerry is not of the class of farmers who report in person for labor in the fields" and, subsequently, discovered that Simpson's friends referred to him as "a farmer by consent for political purposes."[23] In addition, the calm, witty, sagacious image of Simpson as a public figure was never rooted in reality. His debates with his Republican opponents James R. Hallowell and Chester I. Long were vicious and sarcastic, and a sympathetic

Kansas editor who knew Simpson intimately later noted that he had a "combative disposition" and was "not well liked in his home community."[24]

Moreover, Simpson's performance as a public figure was determined by two personality traits which shaped his political behavior. The first, a profound fatalism, was so deeply rooted that he accepted the failure of his cause as an article of faith. "The bitterest thought, and the hardest to bear, is the hopelessness of the struggle, the futility of sacrifice," he confessed in 1889. "But for us who have taken up the crusade, there shall be no halting; and as our ranks grow thin by death and desertion, we should close up, shoulder to shoulder, and show an unbroken line to the enemy."[25] Again, in 1894, he predicted to a sympathetic newspaper that "when times improve, when idle men find employment and better industrial conditions prevail, then the populist party will cease to be. It will have no excuse for living, and it will go out of existence."[26]

Simpson tempered his fatalism with a curious kind of cynicism. "Will you tell me why you are a Populist?" Speaker Thomas B. Reed once inquired of him. "For the same reason," Simpson retorted, "that you are a Republican. A majority of the people of our respective districts are of our way of thinking."[27] Realizing that inertia was the great enemy of reform and convinced that inertia would emerge as the ultimate victor, Simpson permitted himself few illusions. "We reformers are fighting for a mud ball as big as a boulder," he averred in a rare moment of qualified hope. "'What we permanently win will be no larger than a diamond, but it will be a diamond."[28]

Nevertheless, Simpson proved unable to render assistance in the quest for the diamond, largely as a consequence of a second personality trait: his "inability to localize his efforts"[29] and to deal effectively in specifics. Populism was a movement which diagnosed specific maladies and prescribed specific remedies; but Simpson's horizons were too broad, his view of social processes too organically conceived to function effectively in the Populist milieu. He was unsystematic; he tended haphazardly to the needs of his constituents; and his deep fatalism permitted him a kind of political latitude which enabled him to emphasize anything he wished, no matter how peripheral to the basic principles of his party.[30] Because Simpson viewed his efforts as predestined to fail, he regarded his political behavior as immaterial and frequently acted in a manner contradictory to effective third-party action. Therefore, as the unquestioned spokesman for the Populist delegation in the House, his disservice to the cause was unwittingly compounded.

In truth, the "sockless statesman" had no sense of party discipline. The nature of the People's party insured that if discipline was to exist at all, it had to be imposed by the leaders upon themselves; the party organization was too rudimentary and the rank and file too unskilled to force rigid adherence to the root principles of the movement. Simpson, the undisciplined Populist, became a Populist without principle. This statement does not imply a moral or ethical judgement because "without principle," in this instance, means that Simpson treated the basic Populist dogma in a very cavalier manner and that, even on issues of grave concern to him, he rarely possessed the courage of his convictions. These characteristics, hardly unusual in politicians, were highly detrimental to a reform figure representing a third-party movement. David Leahy, a longtime intimate of Simpson, pointed out that an integral facet of his "inability to localize his efforts" was a conviction that "the smaller good was the enemy of the larger good,"[31] that seemingly well-conceived reform objectives would fail to produce permanent improvement unless the totality of society was restructured in the process. Simpson's public behavior from 1891 to 1900 indicates that he regarded most Populist demands—and most Populists—as representative of the "smaller good."

This conclusion does not follow inexorably from a superficial examination of his career, but it does emerge from a detailed comparison of his Kansas and Washington performances and his public posture and private behavior. On the surface Simpson's views on major Populist issues—land, transportation, money, and labor—were standard, explicit, and personally unrevealing. They reflect a syncretism of reform demands from Greenback days to the Alliance, with the notable exception of the sub-treasury scheme for which Simpson apparently had little use. More often than not, however, Simpson's activities were directly contradictory to his public pronouncements.

On the issues of land monopoly and alien land ownership, for example, Simpson was more deeply involved than most Populists because of his devotion to single-tax economics. The present land system, he once complained, was "a robbery,"[32] a denial to the people of access to "the great storehouse of wealth where the God that created this earth stored up enough for everybody. Man is a land animal," he continued; "he can neither live under the earth nor in the earth.... If by granting special laws and legislating special privileges for monopolies you have deprived your brother of a chance to live, he must go back to you and buy the right to live."[33] Yet, in spite of his visceral commitment to land reform, Simpson made little effort in Congress to dramatize the cause except to promote the opening of land in the Cherokee Strip, which happened to border on his district, and to insert single-tax material in the *Congressional Record* as part of a conspiracy with a few other congressmen.[34]

In addition, the problems of transportation and railway chicane in Kansas were so closely tied to land monopoly that Simpson viewed them as indistinguishable. The Santa Fe interests, the "giant spider,"[35] had entangled the Kansas farmer in a web, monopolizing transportation, commerce, and the land mass. But Simpson was less concerned about the railroad problem than many Populists. "We must own the railroads or enough of them to do the necessary carrying," he contended. "'Tis idle talk to say we have not the authority. The government is the people and we are the people."[36] In January, 1893, on the occasion of the inauguration of Lorenzo D. Lewelling as the first Populist governor of Kansas, Simpson told a jubilant crowd gathered on the steps of the statehouse in Topeka that "we have come here today to remove the seat of the government of Kansas from the Santa Fe offices back to the statehouse where it belongs. You have beaten the Santa Fe railroad and you must organize the legislature tomorrow and I wouldn't let the technicalities of the law stand in the way."[37] Eight years later, his public career ended, Simpson moved to New Mexico and secured the agency for the sale of the overpriced lands of the villainous Santa Fe, an ironic ending for a man who had castigated the railroad across the length and breadth of the Big Seventh.[38]

Simpson's views on monetary policy were more refined. Indeed, he was fairly well but not intimately acquainted with monetary theory. A believer in the "gold conspiracy," he nevertheless regarded free silver with great distrust and adhered instead to the fiat money doctrines of his Greenback days. He held the bimetallist notion of compensatory action to be intrinsically absurd, and he scorned international bimetallism as similarly contradictory to "the eternal law of supply and demand" which regulated the value of everything, including precious metals.[39]

Monetary inflation, induced by free coinage of silver or by sub-treasuries, was never especially important to Simpson as a means of enhancing commodity prices. He regarded both as ineffectual panaceas. Money was simply the "representative value of all things," and, as long as society agreed to receive some tangible substance in payment of debts, that substance was acceptable to Simpson. On one occasion, commenting on the futility of coining silver, issuing certificates on the coined metal, and redeeming the certificates in gold, Simpson observed that it would be quite as logical to issue certificates on the precious metals "still in the mountains."[40]

In spite of his distrust of free silver, Simpson was in the vanguard of the Populists who favored the elevation of free silver to the status of the overriding political issue in 1896.[41] But in his own campaign to regain the seat which he had lost to a Republican, Chester Long, in 1894, Simpson refused to focus his campaign on the issue. He discussed monetary policy just enough to prove that such matters were not wholly mysterious to him and conducted the bulk of his campaign as an exercise in invective. Drawn into a series of debates with the incumbent Republican, Simpson merely scoffed at the notion that money derived its value from the "material of its manufacture" and asserted that the "number of dollars compared with the demand for dollars regulates the value of dollars."[42]

Simpson had advocated concentration on free silver and then proceeded to jettison the issue. When Long raised legitimate questions for debate—serious questions such as the efficacy of compensatory action, the effect of free coinage on silver bullion prices, the possibility of retaining gold coins in circulation with unlimited coinage of silver—Simpson provided curt answers devoid of explanation and finally declared that he would waste no more time in answering the incumbent's questions. In sum, he treated the issue with derision.[43] Concerning money, he joked, if people preferred metallic security he would ask "the boys" to appoint a committee to "figger an estimate" on the gold and silver in the mountains "not found." If the circulating media issued on this estimate proved insufficient, "we will give that press ... another whirl and you shall have more on a raised estimate...."[44]

Simpson's views on the general subject of labor, another area of Populist concern, were also in direct contradiction to his actual behavior. Often professing a simple labor theory of value, he claimed to sympathize with the major demands of laboring men—the eight-hour day, prohibition of contract and Oriental labor, immigration restriction, and the proscription of strike-breaking thugs and Pinkerton detectives in labor disputes. In his one experience as a representative of the "employing class," however, Simpson conducted himself somewhat differently.

In the spring of 1888 Simpson, soon to campaign for the Kansas legislature on the Union Labor ticket, submitted the lowest bid on a construction project designed to divert water from a nearby stream into the town of Medicine Lodge. When Simpson was unable to post a small forfeit bond, the contract was awarded to the next lowest bidder, with whom Simpson promptly formed a partnership.[45] The stratagem had probably been prearranged to outmaneuver the town, but this was only a minor ethical oversight. The wage scales were minimal, and the payment was tendered in scrip redeemable at a local store, a practice which prompted many people to surmise that the partners received a drawback from the manager.[46] But Simpson promised to adhere to the "eight-hour system," meaning, as one local newspaper suspected, "work eight hours in the forenoon and eight hours in the afternoon."[47] Angered by public criticisms of his labor policies, Simpson hastily defended his actions in the local press. Low wages, he argued, simply proved that the Republican economic policies had failed to abolish pauper labor. "You cannot reform society by private contributions [wages]," he pontificated,

"...labor being a commodity you buy in the market, and buy as cheap as you can, and the price of labor depends largely on supply and demand."[48] In essence, the system, not Simpson, was to blame.

More important than documenting the self-rationalized inconsistencies and contradictions in Simpson's behavior, however, is the elemental realization that as an elected representative of the Populist party he devoted little effort to promoting the reforms demanded by the party. In Washington Simpson became increasingly temperate, even bland. This was apparent even in his first term. Speaking in New Hampshire as a freshman congressman, he disappointed the Yankees. "Simpson, the Sockless, has come and gone," reported a Manchester paper with mock chagrin. "His speech was evidently carefully prepared with a view to adapt it, so far as possible, to the conservative notions of New England. When Jerry packed his grip to come East, he put in his store clothes, including his socks, and left out most of his patented principles."[49]

Indeed, Congressman Simpson devoted most of his attention to protectionism and militarism. The tariff issue was of very minor concern to the People's party. Although major Alliance organizations had demanded tariff reform in the St. Louis and Ocala platforms, the issue was obscured after 1890, and tariff recommendations did not appear in the Omaha Platform or subsequent statements of party doctrine. Interestingly, a survey of Kansas farmers in 1893 showed that only two of 442 respondents blamed protectionism for their economic problems.[50] Nevertheless, Simpson singled out the protective tariff for special condemnation and stated his views with unmistakable clarity. "I am a free trader in all that the word implies," he told his congressional colleagues. "The right to trade the products of my labor with the man that will give me the greatest return from the products of his labor is one of the rights of the human family, and any law that restrains or abridges that right is an interference with the liberty of the human race."[51] Thus the tariff was a moral outrage, a denial of freedom, and Simpson denounced it primarily in moral terms. It was only incidentally "a fine on trade" and "a primitive form of robbery."[52] Moreover, the tariff was an insult to the intelligence of the American people, for protectionism was predicated on the assumption that they would make bad bargains if left to their own devices. "Is not the Yankee particularly noted all over the world for making smart trades and good bargains?" he asked.[53]

Simpson regarded the economics of protectionism as inherently stupid. Because foreigners were unable to sell in American markets, ships under foreign registry came to American ports in ballast to secure American products for the European markets, forcing American exporters to pay double freight charges.[54] Meeting the argument that the tariff protected American labor, he asked why labor, which "produces all the wealth in the world," should require protection. "Does it not follow ... that labor, the king, labor, the sovereign, has been pushed from his throne where capital now reigns, a bastard monarch, in his stead?"[55] Nevertheless, Simpson was unable to relate the tariff issue to major Populist grievances, and here his organicism curiously failed him. His economic defense of free trade consisted of a naive contrast of British wage levels with wages in the protectionist nations on the continent, which permitted him to conclude that American wage levels would rise if the tariff walls came down.[56]

Like other Populists, Simpson favored an income tax to replace the tariff as the principal source of government revenue. He slyly attributed credit to himself for the income-tax provision of the Wilson-Gorman tariff; but later he reflected some of the credit on the entire Populist delegation, "the ten brave representatives of the interests of the people" who weathered the onslaughts of the "trusts, monopolies and public press [who] with unscrupulous zeal were combined to crush them."[57] When the Supreme Court invalidated the tax in the Pollock case, Simpson blithely declared that he would no longer promote the cause of free trade because revenue had to come from some source![58]

Simpson also attacked bills for military and naval appropriations with some consistency. Unlike an old sailor, he regarded the navy as unnecessary and embarrassing: it "went swaggering around recently and very nearly got us into a difficulty with the little Republic of Chile...."[59] Furthermore, he professed contempt for military pensions, arguing that the pension evil grew out of the use of force to settle disputes, which in turn fostered bonded indebtedness, bureaucracy, and other evils. Children, he reasoned, should be taught that war is cowardly. And, if pensions were justified at all, he concluded, it proved only that an evil plutocracy had denied the people the right to a decent living.[60]

Although Simpson condemned militarism, he did not deny that he had been guilty of "vociferating so loudly for the war" before the outbreak of hostilities with Spain, but he retracted his statements and cast a lonely Populist vote against the war resolution.[61] Subsequently, he opposed a Republican proposal to finance the war effort with a bond issue as another manipulation by the "money power and bondholders of the world," and he also denounced American military activity in the Philippines as imperialism similar to that of other republics in history which had come to possess concentrated wealth.[62]

Significantly, whenever Simpson chose to emphasize a non-Populist issue, such as the tariff in 1894 and imperialism in 1898, his constituents repudiated him. There was an ironic justice in this, since he was often lukewarm to

Populist reform measures. In 1892, for example, the House acted upon the Sherman Grain Grading bill, an "anti-option" proposal which had significant ramifications for Simpson's future relations with his party. The measure proposed a regularization in grading procedures for the five major grains, a reform long desired by prairie farmers. Simpson voted against it and defended his action by explaining that it would introduce government meddling in the grain market without prohibiting the trade in futures. Although this was hardly the intention of the bill, it became obvious to many people in Kansas that Simpson, the "dirt farmer," had confused "grading" with "classification." Through ignorance or misunderstanding he had voted contrary to the interests of his constituents; and when called to account for his action, he weakly explained that the bill had originated with the "millers' trust."[65]

In addition, Simpson was later accused of complicity in lobbying activity in Topeka designed to frustrate the legislative program of the second Populist administration in the state. Early in 1897 two Populist state senators reported that they had been offered bribes if they would withdraw their support for a stockyards bill which had administration blessing. The bill, drafted by officials close to Governor John W. Leedy, proposed to establish maximum rates for feed, yardage, weighing, and watering at Kansas City.[64] One of the senators, Andrew Jackson Titus, later avowed that Simpson was allied with the lobbyists and sympathetic to their intentions. Simpson, however, was never linked to the attempted bribery.[65] Moreover, it was also intimated that Simpson lobbied against the Leedy administration's maximum freight-rate bill. When former Governor Lewelling, then in the state senate, cast his vote against the measure, many Populists concluded that a Simpson-Lewelling faction had coalesced to thwart the governor's program. Simpson denied involvement in the maximum freight-rate episode, but he never commented on the stockyards bill accusation.[66]

When Simpson was consulted on the matter of state appointments and party nominees, he usually urged the selection of non-Populists. In the midst of the Kansas "Legislative War" of 1893, for example, he pressured Populist legislators to make John Martin, a Democrat, the party's choice for senator. Simpson reasoned that Martin would be assured of a seat in Washington, but the rank and file of the party failed to appreciate Simpson's pragmatism.[67] The mere mention of Martin's name at the previous convention had evoked a chorus of "jeers and insults"; and James. B. Weaver, deeply disappointed by the choice, had admonished the party that Martin "should be the last so-called Democrat elected with Populist votes."[68] And, on another occasion, Simpson participated in a stratagem which secured a Senate seat for John M. Palmer of Illinois, who, much to the embarrassment of the Populists, turned up on the Gold Democrat ticket in 1896![69]

Little wonder that Simpson soon provoked opposition from within his party. His attitude toward many Populist principles became a matter of growing concern to the party. And, when his vote on the "anti-option" bill evoked the first doubts about his sincerity, he was publicly reprimanded by a state judge in his district, George Washington McKay.[70] A feud stemmed from this confrontation and simmered for some years, but the cleavage between the Simpson and McKay factions in the party entered the public phase after Simpson regained his House seat in 1896.

McKay and Simpson were among the partners in the Barber County *Index,* a Democratic paper which supported the Populists in the 1890s. Simpson, miffed by the constant sniping of the McKay forces and convinced that the paper's increasingly cool attitude toward him was attributable to McKay's influence with the editor, filed suit against the organ early in 1897, alleging that the paper was so extravagantly operated that his investment was endangered. In McKay's absence a probate judge granted Simpson's petition and appointed a receiver; but McKay soon returned to Medicine Lodge, disposed of his interest in the *Index,* heard the argument, and granted a petition to dismiss the receiver and reinstate the original management.[71] The issue was joined, and the McKay forces sought the assistance of Governor Leedy in their drive to eliminate Simpson as a power in the Big Seventh.

Increasingly, Anti-Simpson men were appointed to strategic positions in the district, but the Congressman was deeply intrenched. By July, 1897, the dispute produced public verbal recriminations. "I don't like Simpson," Judge McKay told a prominent newsman. "He isn't honest. He does not believe what he says or else he goes back on it whenever desirable.... He is a demagogue. He poses as a champion of the people and spends his time in Washington with champagne suppers and high living."[72] In neighboring Harper County the McKay faction won a notable victory when the Central Committee withdrew an invitation to address their convention which Simpson had previously accepted.[73] When the committee met, moreover, he was publicly "impeached."

The articles of impeachment drafted by the Harper County Populists in August 1897 consisted of seven charges. Two of the accusations were concerned with personalities; and one, the assertion that Simpson kept a "jug" of whiskey in his room at Topeka during the 1897 legislative session "contrary to the bottle custom of the short-grass country," was purely peevish. Simpson refused to commit himself on the first two matters, and he defended his choice of whiskey containers with the assertion that the jug contained a quality product and that many Populist leaders had rendered assistance in the consumption of its contents. The remaining four charges were more substantial. Simpson was asked to explain his vote on the "anti-option" bill, his

participation in the Palmer election which obviously contradicted the interests of cheap money, his opposition to the Leedy administration's maximum
freight-rate measure, and his allegedly libelous remarks about Senator Titus.
In an unconvincing performance Simpson denied the libel and lobbying
charges, asserted that "anti-option was bad legislation," and insisted that the
Palmer election was part of a massive trade which secured the reelection of
James H. Kyle in South Dakota, an explanation which Simpson's newspaper
later contradicted.[74] The Simpson faction won a narrow victory, but on the
occasion of his renomination in 1898 only half of the voting delegates were in
their seats.[75]

After his defeat in 1898 Simpson temporarily retired from politics and established his newspaper, *Jerry Simpson's Bayonet.* This scurrilous journal was
appropriately named because Simpson employed its pages to square accounts
with his enemies. Opposed to trusts, militarism, and pensions, the *Bayonet*
also excoriated such conservative leaders as McKinley, Cleveland, Reed, and
former Senator John J. Ingalls of Kansas. Many of the choicest items of disparagement were reserved for Simpson's former Populist comrades. William
A. Peffer, once called a "musty old back number," was frequently abused.[76]
On the occasion of the suicide of Benjamin M. Clover, a Populist congressman
who reverted to Republicanism, the *Bayonet* remembered that he was "scum"
and "decayed tissue."[77] Senator Kyle became "the Kyle creature who sold
himself to Mark Hanna in 1897 in order to secure re-election," a specific contradiction of Simpson's previous explanation of his involvement with Palmer.[78]
And Ignatius Donnelly, who, in spite of a recurrent propensity to hew to the
middle-of-the-road position, agreed with Simpson on nearly everything except
Henry George, received special treatment. The *Bayonet* learned that Donnelly
had responded to a facetious statement that Simpson authored a book entitled
"If the Devil Came to Congress" with the assertion that the devil had already
visited Congress, coming originally "without any socks" and later retiring to
"a large stock farm in Kansas." "Ignatius as usual is off on his facts," the
Bayonet retorted. "If Jerry Simpson ever writes a book it will be entitled
'How the Devil Came to Donnelly, agreed to give him the Presidency and
afterward gave him the loud ha, ha!'"[79]

Reflecting the fall of Simpson's political star, the *Bayonet* quickly experienced financial difficulty. Nevertheless, he developed senatorial aspirations
and labored hard to secure an endorsement at the July, 1900, Populist state
convention.[80] The result was personal humiliation. Though commonplace in
some states, convention endorsements for senator were not employed in
Kansas. Kansas Populists regarded the election of a senator by popularly
elected legislators as closer to the ideal of direct election, an ideal which

Simpson presumably shared with his Populist colleagues. When he sought to add a senatorial endorsement to the agenda, the delegates were furious; and when he tried to bring the matter to the floor on a motion of personal privilege, he was shouted down and denounced as "King."[81] Defeated, he conceded to the convention, "We have met the enemy, and we are his'n."[82] Thomas A. McNeal, a Republican editor and Simpson's erstwhile opponent in the state elections of 1886 and 1888, observed the proceedings from the gallery and concluded that even if the Populists controlled the legislature, Simpson had "no more chance than a fat, asthmatic pug dog in a race with a full grown and active jackrabbit."[83]

Simpson's political career had reached an inglorious climax; the revivalistic milieu which had sustained him in spite of his dubious credentials had vanished by 1900. The tide of "cumulative indignation" which he depicted as the source of Populism had ebbed.[84] He fired a final salvo at the "respectables" of society, condemned them as "conservators of all that is rotten in society," and likened them to "bats, who blink their eyes in the light and flee...when a feeble ray penetrates the cave in which they live with such fellow spirits as brute selfishness, prejudice, sensuality, and a flock of other evil things."[85] In the beginning and in the end, at least, Jerry Simpson was consistent.

CHAPTER THREE
William Vincent Allen: Misplaced Populist

When William Vincent Allen was chosen in 1893 by the Populist-Democratic coalition which dominated the legislature of Nebraska to represent the state in the United States Senate, his election was greeted with approbation by a number of Republican leaders in the state. Edward Rosewater, editor of the conservative Omaha *Bee,* the state's major Republican daily, congratulated the legislature on the wisdom of its choice. Allen, he observed, is not a "hair-brained visionary or wild-eyed revolutionist. Quite the contrary ... he is ... well-balanced, broadminded and *conservative.*"[1] Though such Republican praises could hardly have been reciprocated by Nebraska Populists in 1893, Rosewater's description of Allen's attitudes was correct in every particular and his senatorial performance soon demonstrated it amply.

In fact, Rosewater's observations accurately foreshadowed Allen's eight year career in the Senate. His philosophy, recalled an old friend many years later, "was rather over on the conservative side of the Populist movement,"[2] and Allen himself both preceded and succeeded his senatorial career with long periods of service to each of the established parties. "I was never a radical party man and am not today," he acknowledged shortly after his senatorial career had begun. "I think a party should be held no more sacred than a man's shoes or garments ...."[3]

To put the matter succinctly, Allen, whom many people viewed as the principal intellectual figure which the Populist movement contributed to Federal office, was never really in sympathy with the party's organization and even less so with its reform program. Born in 1847 in Ohio, and reared in a family active in abolitionist circles, Allen was a commonplace participant in the westward movement. In 1857 his family migrated to Iowa, and Allen spent an abbreviated boyhood, ending with successful service as an underaged

---

Facing photograph: William V. Allen, U.S. Senator from Nebraska, 1893-1901. Photo *ca.* 1900. With grateful acknowledgement to the Nebraska State Historical Society.

volunteer in the Union Army and a less successful stay at Upper Iowa College in Fayette. Subsequently, he read law, gained admission to the Iowa bar in 1869, and practiced in the villages of Ackley, Iowa, and Oconto, Wisconsin.[4] But the west soon prevailed, and in 1884 Allen relocated in Madison, Nebraska, alleging that "there is a chance for me to get to the front there and where I propose to be before many years."[5]

Apparently Allen accepted the entire complex of conservative capitalist economic and personal values without reservation. In politics he changed sides as prudence dictated, voting for Tilden in 1876 and running unsuccessfully as a reform Republican congressional candidate in 1878. Badly defeated in the election, he deserted the reform cause and stayed safely within the regular Republican ranks until late in 1891 when he belatedly converted to Alliance views.[6] As late as 1886 he spoke often on such subjects as the "Glorious Republican Party,"[7] and in 1890 he was instrumental in the campaign of the victorious Republican gubernatorial candidate in Nebraska.[8] Hence before 1890 his third party disposition was either latent or altogether dormant.

As a Populist Allen served a full term in the Senate, failed in his re-election bid, and was finally sent back to complete the unexpired term of Monroe Hayward, Nebraska's junior Senator, who died in 1899.[9] Ideologically and personally Allen was uncomfortable in Populist circles, and there was good reason for his reserved and aloof attitude toward his fellow Populists. If reasonably consistent adherence to the fundamentals of the 1892 Omaha Platform provides a basic guide to the commitment of individual Populists, then a comparison of Allen's particular beliefs and inclinations with the Omaha document yields a nearly complete contradiction. Therein lay a very fundamental weakness in the Populist movement—the discrepancy between the party's program and the individualistic behavior of its elected representatives, a structural weakness endemic in the movement which usually vitiated its capacity for effective action. Not only did Allen and other Populists preach differentially, but they failed to practice what they preached.

Though William Jennings Bryan later described him as "the most prominent populist in the United States,"[10] Allen's private views and public performance were a denial of Populist convictions. For Allen accepted none of the Omaha platform except its monetary and coinage sections. He castigated the "sub-treasury" scheme and alleged that no respectable congressman would promote the idea.[11] He was not aggrieved with the behavior of the nation's railways, and he confessed that he was "not especially eager for any large venture into the field of government railroading."[12] Proposals for government ownership of telephone and telegraph facilities left him unimpressed, though he once sponsored a bill for their purchase, and he regarded such political reforms as the referendum and initiative with skepticism. The recall device infuriated him, possibly reflecting his loyalty to the judicial fraternity in which he participated as a district judge for two years before his appointment to the Senate. And, lastly, Allen professed to see that no particular improvement in political morality would result from implementation of the direct primary idea.[13]

In addition, Allen appeared to retain only an indirect and remote relationship with his party organization. Though he was chosen to serve as chairman of Nebraska Populist conventions of 1892, 1894 and 1900, as well as the National Convention of the People's Party in 1896, these functions were ceremonial and represented the exploitation of his judicial experience while removing him from participation in the hard political dealing of the conventions. Silas Holcomb, fusionist (Populist-Democratic) governor of Nebraska (1895-1899), routinely confided in Allen, but the basis of their relationship was personal friendship, not party necessity.[14] Though Allen was a member of the Nebraska Farmers' Alliance, and the Alliance was largely responsible for initiating his public career, he had only the most tenuous contact with the organization. A few of his speeches were sent to Alliance headquarters, but Allen's correspondence with the group was formal, correct and distant.[15] "The Alliance is the cradle of the People's Party," he observed tepidly in 1894, "and it ought not to be permitted to go down."[16]

Again, if the Omaha Platform of 1892 represents a summary of the Populist position, Allen's ideological suppositions and programmatic views coincided with the Omaha document only on matters of coinage and monetary policy. In addition, he shared with many other Populists a disposition toward enhancing the relative power of the states, an explicit but ordinarily unnoticed element in the movement. But, on balance, Allen was no more than a well-grounded and knowledgeable monetary theorist, and he did not hesitate to apprise his colleagues in the Senate of his expertise.

Allen's senatorial career clearly demonstrated his preference for matters of monetary and coinage policy. Protocol notwithstanding, Allen, as a freshman Senator, entered vigorously into the debate provoked by President Cleveland's demand that the Sherman Silver Purchase Act be repealed. Bombastic, ponderous, moralistic, and verbose, Allen's oratory was full of simplistic allusions to patriotism and doled out in amounts consistent with his own physical bulk, which was considerable. In September of 1893, when silverites undertook to filibuster the bill to repeal the Sherman law, Allen lectured his fellow Senators (mostly absent, since he spoke all night) for fifteen hours on the essence of money.[17] He emerged as a competent and thoughtful monetary authority, conversant with the classic works of economic thought, the major British classical economists and the French-Italian bimetallist Henri Cernuschi, but his thought was equally indebted to monetary cranks like the American Edward Kellogg and rested ultimately on the assumption of a gold conspiracy in England and America. It is impossible to escape the conclusion that his thought combined sophistication and conspiracy in approximately equal proportions, and he could quote Adam Smith in one breath and the Winfield (Kansas) *Non-Conformist* in the next as equivalent authorities.[18]

Nevertheless, in modern terms Allen's monetary views were distinctly well-considered and elaborately articulated. Yet in his filibuster performance he probably exhausted his stock of monetary knowledge. At least he never again undertook such an extensive job of monetary enlightenment in the Senate chamber before 1895, when his interests seemed to shift to other matters of policy. Nor did he acquire any new views on monetary policy while in the Senate, and his belief in the existence of a gold conspiracy remained fixed and unchanged.

In brief, Allen's interests were largely related to gold and silver coinage policies in his first years in the Senate, shifted to questions of debt and bond policy after 1894, and his firm belief in the conspiratorial character of both tied his interests together. Basic to his attitudes in the first instance was a severely instrumentalist view of the nature of money, which led him to accept a very pragmatic set of postulates about the material, substance, volume and deployment of money. What most upset him about the monetary views of many in the non-Populist majority, and the matter to which he addressed himself most forcefully, was the notion that money possessed an intrinsic value.[19] Though he had never involved himself with the Greenback movement, he could easily have defended Greenback ideas. He believed in free silver, not for the sake of silver, but because he did not believe in gold, the superior value of gold, or the deflationist-prone interests which he felt gained the most from gold monometallism. He contended flatly that "it is the power or function which performs the office of exchange which makes the money, and not the commercial value of the material which is used in the performance of that function."[20] This was a specific repudiation of the monetary orthodoxy of his day.

The theory of intrinsic value, Allen argued, was put to use in behalf of gold monometallism by deliberate conspiracy of the "Shylocks." "It is only because the volume of gold is scarce, because it is in the grasp of the Shylocks, because they control it and, through it, control the destinies and the progress of the peoples of the earth, that we hear so much about the necessity of sound money ...," he alleged in 1893.[21] If the theory of intrinsic value was abandoned, "the occupation of the money changer, like the occupation of

Othello, is gone."[22] To buttress his own case Allen relied heavily upon authorities. Indeed, he reveled in the citation of authorities, and he brought into use and gave equal credence to Aristotle, Say, Macleod and Henri Cernuschi to disprove the idea of intrinsic value. For good measure he also cited the monetary crank Edward Kellogg, whose *Labor and Other Capital* had once influenced (and helped to destroy) the old National Labor Union.[23]

Secondly, Allen avowed that the deliberate and malicious contraction of the money supply at the instigation of gold monometallists in London and New York was primarily responsible for depressed conditions in the 1890s. Both prosperity and depression were simple functions of the money supply. While the economic evidence for this point of view was circumstantial, he regarded deliberate deflation, beneficial to creditors and bond manipulators, to be the sole reason for declining profits and productivity in both American and European agriculture. The writings of Mill, Ricardo, Smith and Henry Clay provided him with intellectual weapons in his simple explanation of the quantity theory of money.[24] When pointed questions were raised about the correctness of his position, however, he was capable of responding with more than authorities. On one occasion, replying to criticism from a senatorial colleague, he defended himself merely with the assertion "I do not care anything about what the Senator from New Hampshire [Galinger] believes."[25]

Not unrealistically, Allen felt that the money supply should expand with increases in wealth and population, that it should be a reflection of economic growth and commercial needs rather than of arbitrary policy. Unfortunately, his genuine monetary sophistication was offset by his overwhelming obsession with English chicanery. This belief in a gold conspiracy provided Allen with a convenient outlet for a marked and extreme Anglophobia, a constant in his thinking, and at the bottom of the movement against silver in America he detected the presence of English interests intent upon protecting their gold-producing colonies. He observed, "... I see two monster Shylocks, like Argus, hundred-eyed, and, like Briareas, hundred-handed. One of these is England, the other the Shylocks of Wall Street and the East, both alike reaching out their long, bony and merciless hands for their pounds of flesh ...."[26]

This sacrificing of the welfare of the laboring classes could no longer be tolerated, he thought. Again, compounding his allusions to medieval Venice with allusions to Archaic Greece, he asserted that the days of Shylock supremacy were numbered. "We will meet them in Boeotia before they proceed to Attica, and we will not permit them to put the shirt of Nessus on the back of American labor."[27]

By 1895, however, Allen's enthusiasm for silver and general monetary reform had waned, and he redeployed his interests to the related questions of fiscal policy. In reality this shift was merely representative of an extension of his deep convictions. Money — silver, gold, or paper — was merely a technique, an instrument. Underlying money were broader questions of policy and the relationship of group interests to each other in society. Just as free silver would have eased the burdens of laboring men, farmers and debtors in general, after 1895 Allen pursued the same goals by advocating the reform of fiscal policy. Like many Populists, he had a deep, abiding, almost morbid fear of debt. Free silver was an anti-debt technique, but, fiscally speaking, Allen soon found that his adversaries in society regarded debt as a positive good and a desirable element in national policy. Debt, particularly in the form of bonds, comprised "a mortgage upon the property and industry of the producing classes," and the mortgagors were the same goldbug interests who denigrated the silver movement.[28] Thus Allen set out to demonstrate the immorality and self-interested nature of Federal bond policy.

The idea that a national debt was a necessary part of the economic equipment of a mature and sophisticated nation Allen regarded as reprehensible. Bonds were merely a device to transfer money from the laboring, taxpaying members of society to the "money power" with the government serving as a willing middleman in the process. At the same time bonds afforded a safe, profitable and convenient outlet for the surplus funds of the "money power," funds which the "money power" exacted from the unwitting people and which should have been employed for social purposes. With money safely invested in the form of bonds, deflation was enhanced, and the "money power" — "that class of persons who control the great debt, stocks and mortgages of this country and of Europe ... and ... who are directly interested in instantly appreciating money" — profited further.[29] To demonstrate the existence of this money power, Allen felt, it was merely necessary to observe the web of international banking connections and the simultaneity and complementarity of financial panics in England and America.[30] Emerging clearly from his analysis was an old American dualism, perhaps best articulated by Thorstein Veblen, the division of society into two groups, the producers, who are good, and the non-producers, who survive by manipulation.

Aside from matters of monetary and fiscal policy Allen had little interest in economics and probably failed to comprehend how the institutions of a modern economy functioned in tandem. His tariff views, for example, were ambivalent and betrayed a conclusion that the financial community was autonomous and somehow unrelated to the production of tangible goods. This was surely incongruous with his pro-producer biases, and it was precisely this functional conception of the totality of the economic process which Allen, as compared with men like Jerry Simpson, failed to understand. The "mother of trusts" did not elicit Allen's interest, and if he ever perceived a relationship between the tariff, the expansion and contraction of trade, the opening and closing of foreign markets, foreign exchange, monopoly, and the money power he failed to express it publicly. Since the tariff was never a vital area of Populist concern, however, Allen perhaps merits some forgiveness for his stand on the issue. Yet all that he could discern about the tariff was that prosperity had characterized America during periods of both low and high tariff policies. Therefore, prosperity and depression were related solely to the money supply.[31]

While economic matters were Allen's principal interest, he also addressed himself over the years to a number of other disharmonies and problems in America. Probably no aspect of his non-economic thinking was as important or conspicuous as his notion that the People's Party was anointed to abolish sectionalism from America. "In the populist party we know no north, no south, no east, no west ... I thank God it was one of the missions of this great party to destroy sectionalism," he proclaimed in 1896.[32] Inverting historical reality with abandon, he viewed even the Civil War as a mere lovers' quarrel, a temporary estrangement.[33] While Allen perceived a growing hostility between East and West in the nation, he felt that the Populists, with no ties to the sectional animosities of the past, could effectively counterbalance this growing division by promoting a North-South rapprochement.[34] His own activities, however, probably failed to advance the cause materially, and, in any case, he never elaborated his views with consistency or thoroughness. On at least one occasion, moreover, he provoked considerable displeasure among southern Democrats by taking the lead in a move to investigate electoral fraud in Alabama. This projected probe represented the culmination of efforts by Alabama Populists and their recognized leader, Rueben F. Kolb, to draw national attention to the circumstances by which Kolb was denied the governorship in 1892 and 1894. The problem in Alabama, which involved both allegations of a fraudulent tally and the absence of any legal means to contest election results, was eagerly seized upon by Allen, a strong partisan of a "free ballot and a fair count," who transformed the matter into an issue with broader ramifications than Rueben Kolb's failure to secure the Alabama governorship. Ponderously, heavy-handedly, and in a manner calculated to convey insult, Allen raised the question of whether a republican form of government existed in Alabama, and he sponsored numerous resolutions to inquire into congressional contests, the election of state officials and the selection of Senators by the Alabama legislature. These efforts availed nothing, except to alienate southern Democrats and probably to retard Populist-Democratic fusion efforts among the agrarian interests in other southern states.[35]

Moreover, in the Senate Allen demonstrated a small, penurious side to his personality, a characteristic common enough among Populist officials. Just as Jerry Simpson delighted in picking apart pension requests and minor items of military expenditure, Allen, alleging that "the place for reform is at home," undertook in 1895 a bitter attack on the operation of the Senate restaurant. This facility, it seemed, was operated by a private contractor for personal profit, but it used freely provided government space, fuel, ice, furniture, stoves and refrigeration equipment and thus represented a serious misallocation of public funds.[36] Secondly, Allen's most extensive correspondence with the Nebraska Farmer's Alliance concerned the equitable distribution of his annual allotment of twenty packets of garden seeds, and he took some pains to caution that the seeds must be distributed on the basis of loyalty to the Alliance and that no family receive more than one packet![37]

By 1895, the year in which Allen interested himself in the allegations of election fraud in Alabama and the gratuitous terms which underlay the dispensing of the senatorial cuisine, his interests had begun to shift away from the domestic concerns which ordinarily provoked Populist analysis to the large questions of foreign policy thrust suddenly into prominence by the eruption of revolution in Cuba. He quickly forsook his role as Populist gadfly for that of independent statesman, though his foreign policy attitudes were remarkably uncomplex and inflexible. He was an aggressive and self-righteous expansionist, provocative in utterance and bellicose in attitude. No other Senator was able to state so forthrightly in March of 1898, "Mr. President I am the jingo of jingoes."[38]

Allen was especially interested in Cuba and in American policy toward the unhappy island. He was among the first in Congress (December, 1895) to press for American recognition of the belligerent status of the Cuban insurrectionaries, and he repeated his demands on numerous subsequent occasions.[39] As early as February of 1897 he proposed a resolution to dispatch battleships to Cuban waters, partly to secure the liberty and property of American citizens resident on the island but also to compel the Spanish to conduct their military operations on "principles of civilized warfare." And in a major address delivered early in 1898 he asserted that "we stand to Cuba as an elder brother ... we are the guardians of liberty on this continent."[40] But he had no strong party or committee position to lend substance to his words and to hasten the course of American involvement in the increasingly complicated Cuban situation.

Allen's interest in Cuba involved both a moralistic and an economic dimension. He was interested in exporting American political institutions *and* the products of American farms to the island. The expansion of agricultural exports to Latin America, beginning with the penetration of the Cuban market, offered a solid opportunity for the United States to extricate itself from dependence upon the British money lords who, he alleged, dictated American commercial and currency policies. For this reason his aggressively expansionist views knew no limitations, and he advocated a Pan-American Union with a common silver coinage. He was unaware that some of the potential by-products of commercial expansion might be morally and commercially deleterious to the Populist constituency and its world-view, and he was surely the last Populist to confront and accept the jolting reality that the McKinley administration might well turn Cuban affairs over to American financiers. Ultimately he was forced to accept this contention, which had long been held by many other Populists, and he reverted to a posture of exclusive emphasis on the necessity of securing purely *political* independence for the beleaguered Cubans while professing to be pessimistic about the economic effects of that independence.[41]

In addition, his foreign policy attitudes were not altogether consistent, and his early and consummate jingoism failed to obscure obvious blind spots in his outlook. On the one hand, Allen regarded the military behavior in Cuba of the Spanish general Victoriano Weyler, especially his infamous "reconcentration" policy, as brutish and degraded,[42] but he had no difficulty at all in discounting the evidence of Weyler-like treatment by Americans of Filipino insurrectionaries.[43] As a righteous total patriot, he regarded Americans as incapable of doing evil abroad. Since he admitted that Americans were in the Philippines in the role of conquerors, however, he did not approve of American policy there. Yet his moral discomfort could be eased by extending the rights of American citizens to the natives, and he urged that this course of action be followed. In the long run, he felt, the beneficent effect of American institutions would prevail over all obstacles. And in his thinking about the Philippines and Cuba he was absolutely insistent that any new governments established under American auspices adhere to republican principles.[44]

It is a reasonable supposition that by 1895 Allen had grown weary of Populism. The progress of the party did not meet with his earlier expectations, the projected inroads into the major party's power bases did not materialize, and the poor showing of Populist candidates in 1894, especially in Nebraska, deeply distressed him. Hence the role of Senator as Senator became more consequential than the role of Senator as an agent of Populist ideology. Increasingly, Allen concerned himself with what a later critic called "his oppressive, not to say appalling, dignity."[45] A powerless representative of a declining movement after 1896, Allen was in a real sense a long-term lame-duck.

In the course of time Allen became increasingly cynical about the American political process and increasingly disturbed by its products. This was, in part, the natural result of the way in which the system handles its outsiders, and Allen was always an outsider. "I don't know about this senatorial life...," he wrote to his wife in 1900. "One has to work like a negro and do the best he can. The ignorance of the world is appalling and it is doubtful if after all self government will prove a success. The people are daily robbed and do not know it. They can be humbugged and cajoled and seem to like it ...."[46]

Though Allen grew increasingly frustrated in the Senate and eventually came to doubt the usefulness of public service, he experienced some revival of the old Populist faith once he was safely out of office and reestablished in his Madison, Nebraska, law practice. In 1903, in one of the last formal Populist testaments, he professed to see American society as he had a decade earlier. The nation was still sick, he thought, because its monetary system was unreformed, its corporate interests still commanded unquestioned obedience, and its bonding system exploited the laboring classes. Furthermore, injunctions were casually employed to suppress labor, railroad problems were unresolved, aliens owned large blocks of American land, the press filled the people's minds with "European [i.e. English] ideas of government," and the government was guilty of "constant toadying ... to European powers."[47] The Republicans were unwilling, and the Democrats unable, effectively to deal with the problems of the society. Indeed, Allen himself failed to notice many of these problems while serving in the Senate. A year later he announced his entry into the Democracy, and in 1911 he was elected as a Democratic district judge and ended his public career where it had begun, on the bench.[48]

In conclusion, Allen was a rather tragic and certainly misplaced figure. An effective third-party politician of necessity needs some of the characteristics of a firebrand, but Allen's personality was basically judicial, legalistic and dependent upon ultimate notions of authority. His energies and capacities, which were considerable, were also circumscribed by his myopia and his inveterate pomposity. Even within the constricted sphere of his operations, Populism to him was never a creed but an intellectual exercise, sometimes no more than a cerebral reflex. To Allen his party was indeed as expendable as his shoes and garments, not so much because it was an ineffective instrument to disseminate the truths it had discerned, but because Allen did not accept the truths in the first place. Except for his role as a theoretician of monetary policy, William Vincent Allen was a non-Populist. He did not, in short, serve the cause with anything like the expected degree of commitment.

CHAPTER FOUR
Lorenzo D. Lewelling: Incomplete Humanist

Of all the Populist figures who served in high elective office in the 1890s, few if any had the background, inclination, preparation for social reform, experience with the products of social debilitation, and intrinsic decency of character as Lorenzo Dow Lewelling, first Populist governor of Kansas. Lewelling was an unusual Populist—a youthful wanderer, a product of old Quaker stock, a son of abolitionists, a career penal administrator. He was squarely within the Quaker tradition of reformism and social concern, and he had the sophistication and presence of mind to realize it, if not always to act upon it.

Born in 1846 in the little Quaker frontier colony of Salem, Iowa, the son of an abolitionist lecturer who died on the circuit, Lewelling had a rich and varied early life. Before 1872, his twenty-sixth year, he had been a soldier in an Iowa regiment, a bridge-construction worker in both Tennessee and Iowa, an employee of a firm supplying cattle to the Army of the Tennessee, a towpath boy on the Erie Canal, a section-hand on both the Burlington and Union Pacific railways, a student and graduate of a business college in Poughkeepsie, New York, and of Whittier College in Salem, Iowa, a carpenter in Ohio and a teacher in both Missouri and Iowa as well as the editor of the weekly Salem *Register*.[1] Settling down in Iowa after 1872, Lewelling developed an interest in social phenomena, and though he professed to be a Republican in Iowa, he later confessed that his experiences were such that "the seed was sown which afterwards resulted in my conversion."[2]

For most of the fourteen years between 1873 and 1887 Lewelling and his wife fulfilled the roles, in present-day terms, of penologist and institutional social worker in the service of the state of Iowa. As superintendent and matron of the Girls Division of the Iowa Reform School, the Lewellings held their positions at Mt. Pleasant with only a brief interlude until the death of

Facing photograph: Lorenzo Dow Lewelling, with grateful acknowledgment to The Kansas State Historical Society, Topeka, Kansas.

Mrs. Lewelling and the removal of her husband to Kansas. In this period his reports pertaining to the operation and function of the Girls Division were revealing of his attitudes and demonstrated that his ultimate commitment to an avowedly reformist party was not the result of a late conversion. Lewelling was a life-long observer and astute analyst of social malaise and human degradation, and his recommendations and comments on penal procedure represented a sociological comprehension of modern dimensions. "It is best," he once said of his problem cases, "to deal gently with the erring, for too often their evil habits are but the unwelcome heritage bequeathed by a vicious and depraved parentage."[3]

In his biennial reports he spoke of the ideal of a "perfect reformatory," based on the principle of the family as a microcosm of society.[4] Laissez-faire thought, built on the assumption of an individual's total responsibility for his own personality formation and behavior, struck Lewelling as evil and contradictory to the reality of the social processes which made his kind of work necessary. His wards, he often reminded Iowa officials, are "girls from the slums of our cities and all from broken homes where the sweet, quiet influence of love is never known. Of course the progeny of such homes and such circumstances are often shiftless, incorrigible and vicious."[5]

Even at an early stage in his career Lewelling was a sociological "modern." The social processes which produced the alienated and the criminal were life-long concerns, and even as governor of Kansas he sometimes corresponded with penitentiary inmates and their wives about pardons, preferring to see the mitigating circumstances in individual cases and professing to believe that proper social circumstances would supply all of the corrective influences necessary for self-reformation.[6] As an act of gubernatorial good faith, for example, he routinely pardoned all inmates just prior to the expiration of their terms in order to restore their civil liberties and suffrage rights.[7]

In the spring of 1887, at the height of the boom which collapsed so dramatically later in the year, Lewelling left Iowa for the flourishing town of Wichita and became a partner in a commission firm dealing in butter, eggs and other farm produce. Before 1887 Lewelling had interested himself in Grange matters, and, during a brief absence from the Girls Department, had edited a reform Republican paper, the Des Moines *Capital.* But he was not a third-party activist and showed no sign of third-party proclivities until the Kansas boom came to such an inglorious end and hardship was evident all around him. Slowly and imperceptibly he moved into harmony with the Alliance position, and by 1890 he emerged as Chairman of the People's Party Committee in Sedgwick County. Reform, given his background, was natural enough.[8]

Fate, not reputation or demonstrated competence, propelled Lewelling suddenly into the administrative matrix of the Kansas governorship, where he lasted for a single term. The rather natural choice of Wichita, in the heartland of Populism, as the site of the 1892 People's Party convention, Lewelling's function as official host, the enthusiastic response to his well-executed address, the lack of strong alternative contenders—all combined to make him the gubernatorial nominee. His election, given the seething discontent in Kansas, was no surprise, but the margin of his victory was narrow and the composition of the legislature elected at the same time was a matter of dispute.[9]

Lewelling's thinking in 1892 and later proceeded from several assumptions about the polarization of American society. As the dimensions of his thought were revealed in various addresses of his campaign and the early phase of his governorship, it became obvious that he looked at society's problems as a series of elemental dichotomies: individual rights and property rights, masses and classes, the powerful and the powerless, the producers and the manipulators, Federal encroachment and state prerogatives, West and East, good and evil, the corporations and the people.[10] Yet with bluntness and clarity he announced in his inaugural address that the "survival of the fittest is the government of brutes and reptiles," and that government plainly owed its first duty to the weak and unfortunate. "Government," he asserted with obvious Jeffersonian overtones, "is a *voluntary* union for the common good. It guarantees the individual life, liberty and the pursuit of happiness .... If the government fails of these things ... it ceases to be of advantage to the citizen; he is absolved from his allegiance and is no longer held by the civil compact."[11]

For the most part, however, Lewelling's political views consisted of simple aphorisms. It was the function of government to protect "producers" from the "ravages" of combined wealth, the interests of East and West diverged until the McKinley tariff "culminated in their divorcement"; and "we have so much regard for the rights of property that we have forgotten the liberties of the individual."[12] His political philosophy was less developed than his thought about social deviance, and there appears in his papers and his utterances no special hierarchy of grievances, no particular devil-in-chief. The "system" was merely generalized, and its most damaging ramifications were apparent in the West. Lewelling, in fact, was more adept at asking questions than at suggesting solutions. "What is the State to him who toils," he wondered, "if labor is denied him and his children cry for bread?"[13]

Lewelling's prescription for the ills of state and nation was incomprehensible. In large measure it involved an intrusion of conscience into public affairs and little else. Whatever ramifications conscience might have had in inducing legislatively derived social and institutional change is impossible to discern, for the Lewelling administration never had a chance. Thus such memorable remarks as "if old men go to the poorhouse and young men go to prison something is wrong with the economic system of the government" were in reality nothing but pure conjectures.[14]

Lewelling was not, by any utilitarian standards, a successful governor. Like his contemporary, Davis Waite of Colorado, Lewelling faced a hostile legislature, though in Kansas the legislature was first unworkably indeterminate and then finally hostile. The Kansas "Legislative War" of 1893, in which rival Populist and Republican aspirants contended for legitimacy as the legal House of Representatives, was partly vicious and partly comic relief.[15] But the "War" did take up most of the legislative time in the 1893 session and ended effectively any hope Lewelling might have entertained for legislative achievement. Yet it is doubtful that tangible results would have resulted no matter how favorable the circumstances. For Lewelling, like so many other Populists, defined his commitments vaguely, leaving considerable latitude for deviation from common party positions.

Except to suggest the desirability of electoral reform, a strengthened railroad commission, a coal screening (i.e., weighing) law to protect the interests of the state's miners, and mortgage regulation, Lewelling did not present a program to Kansas. That "conscience was in the saddle" appeared to be rationale enough.[16] Nor did he exhibit much interest in, or seek contact with, Populists outside of Kansas, and there is no evidence to indicate that he regarded the People's Party as a long-run reform vehicle or that the Omaha Platform was a major statement of belief which necessitated a personal commitment. Technical matters of policy also failed to elicit his interest. For example, he wrote that the Populists were a "silver party" but that the "philosophy of populism is the philosophy of greenbackism."[17] Questions of fiscal policy might be handled quite nicely, he thought, if governments simply acted upon the motto that "out of debt is out of danger."[18]

But Lewelling's devotion, integrity and decency toward people cannot be doubted. Hard decisions which produced unpleasantness or personal hardship were not among his talents, and he handled appointments and dismissals badly. Besides the disastrous and unworkable legislative situation in Kansas, Lewelling's effectiveness was further reduced by his unfortunate appointments, ineptitude and disloyalty in the state agencies and the party ranks, and the necessity to devote an inordinate amount of time to the enforcement of Kansas' severe and restrictive sumptuary laws.

Perhaps his major drawback was simply that many hard-line (mid-road) Populists, noting the governor's easy adherence to the idea of fusion and his frequent appointment of Democrats, felt that Lewelling took his Populism too lightly. His disdain for ordinary party nomenclature, for example, probably won him few friends. "I am not a stickler for the name of Populist or People's Party," he said in 1893, "it makes little difference what name is assumed ... so that we obtain the results sought."[19] On the other hand, he was a "stickler" for rigid adherence to legalisms, and he often suffered for this attribute by appearing to be a brusque and unfeeling bureaucrat.

Even after the ludicrous "Legislative War" had come to an end, the Lewelling administration had to face difficulties with state personnel of major proportions. At least half of Lewelling's correspondence was concerned with resignations, dismissals and appointments, and the incidence of personnel turnover extended long beyond the organizational phase of the administration. When his administration was scarcely a month old, for example, he found it necessary to remove the entirety of his own Board of Public Works, and this was only the beginning.[20]

Lewelling's most frustrating problems were associated with the people responsible for the enforcement of sumptuary legislation, particularly the Kansas Prohibition law, an activity which consumed large amounts of time and effort and yielded indeterminate results. He knew too much about deviant behavior to believe that prohibition meliorated social evils, but prohibition was law and this was sufficient to produce total commitment to do his "plain duty."[21] Considering that the Police Commissions of the major municipalities in Kansas were gubernatorial appointments and that most of the major cities were adjacent to the "wet" state of Missouri, it was not surprising that the governor's record of administration in these matters was a long, dreary series of dismissals, resignations, rumors and recriminations, while public support for his efforts was minimal.

Nearly as serious were Lewelling's problems with his appointees to the state administrative agencies, some of whom apparently worked at cross-purposes to the governor. Perhaps the most noticeable evidence of these problems was the relationship of Lewelling with Mary Elizabeth Lease, whose original appointment as Chairman of the State Board of Charities represented a political necessity. By November, 1893, a serious rift developed between the two, owing to the incompatibility of the middle-of-the-road and fusionist points of view of the adversaries on such concrete matters as appointments, plus a generous infusion of complicated personality problems. Lewelling's patience was strained to the point that he found it necessary to get Mrs. Lease out of his thinning hair, and, as a kind of belated Christmas present, he informed her in late December, 1893, that "you are to-day removed," citing only the "interests of the Board"[22] as the reason. Vicious interchanges and recriminations followed, and Mrs. Lease was eventually preserved in her position by the State Supreme Court. Irreparable damage was done to the party in Kansas, and this exposure of an unprotected flank within his own party surely contributed to Lewelling's defeat in 1894.[23]

Lewelling, rebuked by the legislature and by a sizeable constituency in his own party, lapsed into a period of inactivity coupled with frequent absences from Topeka. Even his natural inclinations unwittingly made him new enemies. On one occasion, for example, he took the opportunity afforded by a request for assistance in the establishment of a militia company at a little Kansas college to condemn the military tradition. "I am really not in sympathy with keeping alive the military spirit among our young men," he declared, and he further indicated that he planned to recommend a denial of funds for the continuance of the National Guard in Kansas.[24]

Occasionally, however, such problems as strikes and generalized labor conflict aroused him from his lethargy. His personal support for laboring men was complete and instantaneous. In a coal miners' strike at Weir City, Kansas, in July of 1893, for example, he defended the excesses of the miners on the grounds that the operators were even less scrupulous than the miners in their tactics, and he refused to dispatch state troops to the strike scene or to provide state arms to the local sheriff.[25] In July, 1894, moreover, when 500 men commandeered a Missouri, Kansas and Texas railway freight near Salina, in an act inspired by sympathy with the Pullman boycott, Lewelling rejected the pleas of the road's president to use the state militia to retrieve the train.[26]

In addition, the Kansas governor's response to the problems generated by the Pullman boycott in Kansas was revealing of a little noticed component of *ante-bellum* type states' rights postulates in a new and modern form. As a pragmatic tactic, however, Populist believers in states' rights did not advocate nullification of legislative enactments but opted instead for the idea of interposition of state power to block Federal judicial power. John Peter Altgeld's blistering response to the Cleveland administration's handling of Pullman problems in Illinois is a famous episode, but it was bland in comparison with Lewelling's rejoinder to Federal intrusion into Kansas affairs at the same time and for the same reasons. Injunctions issued by Federal courts and made applicable to the Kansas situation were "usurpations" of constitutional state authority and could not meet a constitutional test, he declared. Federal judges, he charged, were responsible for "indignities to sovereign states," the state executive authority was illegally "thrust aside" by the Federal injunctions, and under the terms of these decrees "mercenary retainers of certain railroad companies" overran the state, clearly violating the Federal constitution's provision which grants to the executive and the legislature the exclusive power to raise and equip an armed force.[27]

Nevertheless, if Lewelling was caustic and specific in his attack on judicial power, he was timid in facing his own state legislature. One session with the Kansas legislature had rendered him ineffective, and he was unwilling to face the same legislature a second time. Though Kansas Populists desperately wanted a new railroad regulatory law, and though the summer of 1893 found Kansas farmers suffering terrible hardship from drought, Lewelling rebuffed all demands to call the legislature into session to deal with railroad matters or with the question of relief for the parched western counties.[28] In fact, it was the Alliance, spokesman for the exploited farmers, which most strenuously recommended to Lewelling the inadvisability of a special session and thus turned a deaf ear to the cries for help emanating from western Kansas. Alliance officials were *more* afraid that the Republicans would make the Populist leaders appear to be foolhardy parliamentary amateurs than it was solicitous for the welfare of drought-stricken comrades in the western counties.[29] The Alliance prevailed with Lewelling, and the governor contended that if he called the legislature to consider the matter of relief eastern papers would pick up the story "and come out in glaring headlines about poverty and destitution in Kansas"[30] and that this would impede the future recruitment of settlers. Precisely why, when the population already resident in western Kansas could not be sustained there, Lewelling was so concerned with future population increments is impossible to discern. "After all," he concluded, "we are compelled to adopt methods which are business-like, which is another name for heartlessness, in dealing with each other."[31]

Requests for relief poured in from western Kansas during the summer and autumn of 1893. Overflowing with sympathy for the plight of the farmers, Lewelling would not make a move to give his sympathy a material basis. Untutored farmers, native born and immigrant, candidly explained their plight to the governor on soiled and stained scraps of paper. From Ellis County an old farmer lamented that "our people bought in our township they are put-near all sufering if we dont git any help."[32] The problem, wrote another western Kansan, "is *how to* live."[33] Others pleaded for tax relief or suggested that farmers be allowed to spend their tax contributions for seed, but any proposal which involved dealing with the legislature found Lewelling unresponsive.[34]

In fact, Lewelling was far more congenial to the needs of the town and city laborers of eastern Kansas, a section of the state which did not vote the Populist ticket. Professing that he wished "to do all I am able to alleviate the conditions of the working people of this state," he found some novel and inexpensive ways to assist once the depression of the 1890s seriously affected the Kansas economy.[35] To the Police Commissions of Kansas cities, for example, he suggested that priority in hiring be given to heads of families and that positions be made available in "some instances" by dismissing single men.[36] Moreover, seeing that the depression produced groups of men who moved from place to place in search of employment, men who were classified as ordinary vagrants under Kansas law, Lewelling acted to guarantee them humane treatment and issued to the municipal police commissions of Kansas his notable "Tramp Circular" on December 4, 1893.[37]

The "Tramp Circular," an executive letter which demonstrated mature sociological comprehension and gained for Lewelling a short-lived national reputation, was an order to distinguish between the unemployed and ordinary "tramps" in applying the vagrancy law in Kansas cities. The right to move from place to place, even on a whim, was fundamental, and such exploitative practices as consigning the vagrant unemployed to labor in the "geological department" (i.e., rock pile) must cease. "In this country," Lewelling declared, "the monopoly of labor saving machinery and its devotion to selfish instead of social use, have rendered more and more human beings superfluous." Kansas' vagrancy statutes, by treating the penniless as criminal, have affected "thousands of men, guilty of no crime but poverty, intent upon no crime but that of seeking employment," and allowed them to languish in city prisons or "toil on 'rock piles' as municipal slaves, because ignorance of economic conditions has made us cruel." Once incarcerated, the poor were unable to "litigate with their oppressors" and were denied a voice "because it is nobody's business to be his brother's keeper." Among the "heinous crimes" which one could commit in Kansas, Lewelling said in disbelief, was "sleeping in a boxcar." Finally, and masterfully, Lewelling wrote that "the first duty of government is to the weak. Power becomes fiendish if it be not the protector and sure reliance of the friendless ..." Vagrancy statutes as applied in Kansas were, in Lewelling's estimation, a denial of the equal protection of the laws, and the immediate remedy was simple enough: "Let simple poverty cease to be a crime."[38]

The commentary provoked by the "Tramp Circular" clearly enhanced Lewelling's reputation. Much of the response was hostile and distorted the content of the circular, but the governor's private mail was emotionally gratifying. Supporters, including many unemployed, sent letters of appreciation from every corner of the nation, but a native Kansan provided a eulogy with universal ramifications. "May our heavenly father in his infinite mercy bless you," he implored. "Don't be discouraged, dear governor, because of the miserable howl of the Satanic, plutocratic, abominable, low-down, subsidized republican and democratic money sheets that are paid to abuse you. They are hired wailers—hired mourners—calamity howlers paid for howling."[39] Kansas police commissions, on the other hand, handled the governor skillfully, assuring him that his views were shared by all in official capacities and that his recommendations had been in effect even before he offered them.[40]

It must be pointed out that the recommendations of the "Tramp Circular" were not accompanied by the slightest hint that the state's funds would be available for the municipalities serving as hosts to the indigent unemployed. Cities like Wichita, which provided meals for the transients, did so with no prospect of financial assistance from the Lewelling administration. In a sense, then, the "Tramp Circular" was an expression of humaneness on the cheap. Lewelling, like so many other Populists, apparently saw no connection between the power of sympathy and the power of the public purse as a relief device. His unwillingness to commit resources to alleviate the distress of the unfortunate betrayed the incompleteness of his humanitarian ideals. Apparently he believed the state and the citizenry should not be of concern to each other.[41]

Even a perceptive man like Lewelling, therefore, was guilty of a major discrepancy between attitudes and behavior. This became even clearer when, after his defeat in 1894, he went into the state Senate and served with some distinction until his premature and untimely death in 1900. On the one hand, during his Senate years he allowed himself to be coopted by the reactionary powers he had once opposed, and he became a land agent for the corporation which was most prominent in the demonology of Kansas Populism — the Atchison, Topeka and Santa Fe Railroad.[42] (Jerry Simpson later formed the same connection with the railroad.) On the other hand, his political philosophy moved sharply to the left, and in 1900 he repudiated his old Populist comrades and supported the Socialist candidate for governor. "The Socialist principles are much superior in many respects to the Populists',"[43] he declared, and just before his death he allegedly observed, "I have always had socialist tendencies. So have we all. We must come to it."[44]

In background and temperament Lewelling was a peculiar and distinctive addition to Populist circles. His contact with agrarianism was slight — his forebears were prominent in the nursery stock business and he himself had been a "middleman" in the farm produce business, an occupation farmers had some reason to dislike. His close associates regarded him as personally too gentle to accept the harsh realities of political life, and this trait perhaps diminished his effectiveness. Yet his career was largely a projection of the humanistic background and principles to which he had been born and bred. He thought and reflected often upon social processes, but he did not comprehend that government and its powers might be a deployable force to bring substance and concreteness to his political philosophy.

CHAPTER FIVE
Davis Hanson Waite: The Left Wing

Among the states which produced a Populist movement of significant proportions in the 1890s, Colorado's Populism belongs to the special and distinctive mountain genre. That is, the primary motivation for reform in Colorado derived from factors other than agricultural exploitation and such agricultural problems as alien land ownership, transportation and marketing monopoly, and the absence of credit facilities to serve the agricultural community. Colorado's position as a producer of silver dictated its reform needs, and in the course of time the silver movement became both an article of faith and an agent of survival.[1] In this sense, then, silver dominated mountain state Populism, converting it into a more limited phenomenon than the collateral species of Populism in the plains states and in the South.

Colorado, like Kansas, experienced a major boom in the 1880s, a boom which culminated in absurd optimism, speculative excesses, and ultimately in widespread ruin and deprivation. The in-movement of population was considerable, and Denver, like Wichita, tripled in size during the decade. Unlike Kansas, however, Colorado's development was more lopsided, and the state became an economic colony dominated by eastern corporate interests. Mining, and, to some extent, the cattle industry, were dominated by eastern corporations—by classic absentee landlords. The mining of precious metals, easily the dominant form of enterprise in the Colorado economy, determined the economic health of the state. Falling silver prices, which brought hardship to mine laborers and Eastern slope farmers alike, produced Colorado's peculiar variant of political protest.[2] Unlike the Populist upheaval on the plains, Colorado Populism took on some of the attributes of a genuine proletarian uprising, some characteristics of class warfare.[3] Thus the expected salutary effect of bimetallism on the depressed economy of the state dictated the character of the Colorado People's Party, while the remainder of the elaborate Populist

Facing photograph: Davis Hanson Waite, with grateful acknowledgment to the Denver Public Library, Western History Department.

platform worked out at Omaha was largely excess baggage.[4] One Colorado
Populist, however, proved to be an exception to silver-mindedness and silver
dominance.

Davis Hanson Waite (1825-1905), an Old Yankee of Welsh stock whose
family roots in the New World extended back to 1660, was fated to superin-
tend Colorado's unique onslaught against the prevailing capitalist order in the
state. Born in Jamestown, New York, lawyer, teacher, school principal, superintendent of schools, abolitionist, prospector, editor of three newspapers, and
politician in two states, Waite's long life was a continuous expression of physical, occupational, philosophical and political wanderlust. Formed in the
political crucible of latter-day Jacksonianism, Waite cast his first vote for the
Free Soil party and logically moved into the Republican camp, voting a
straight party ticket until 1892. As his occupation changed frequently, so did
his residence, and he turned up in Fond du Lac, Wisconsin in 1850 as a mer-
chant, stayed there for seven years, served a term in the state legislature, and
departed for Missouri to teach school. By 1860 his abolitionist views made
continued residence there imprudent, and he moved back East, accepting a
post as principal of a high school in Warren, Pennsylvania. Soon he was back
home in Jamestown, tending to a law practice and later undertaking the edi-
torship of two Republican newspapers. But the West won out, and by the end
of the 1870s Waite found his way to Leadville, Colorado, where he engaged in
the dual professions of lawyer and prospector. In 1881 he made his last move,
taking residence in the remote mining town of Aspen and sustaining himself
and his family with a law practice, an appointment as justice of the peace,
and the county superintendency of schools. Aside from his professional
duties he found time to participate in Knights of Labor activity, to serve as
president of the Aspen Trades Assembly, and finally to establish and edit
another newspaper.[5]

In Aspen Waite's political philosophy evolved and matured. Expressed in
the pages of his last newspaper venture, Waite detailed the postulates of his
newly found faith to a small band of readers insulated in the mountain fast-
nesses of the high Rockies. The Aspen *Union Era* (1891-1892) established his
reputation in Populist circles and provided the vehicle for the views which
carried him into the governorship. A stern and unyielding moral purist, Waite
converted Populism into a personal creed, a substitute for the formalized
Christianity which he rejected with easy contempt. Basic to his thought and
providing a firm emotional undergirding for all of his views, was an overwhelming obsession with monopoly. Just as Jerry Simpson developed an obsession with the tariff system and William Vincent Allen was obsessed with
monetary policy, Waite concerned himself with the multivarious facets of

monopoly, and nearly everything Waite saw in American life was a manifestation of monopoly. "Monopoly is the great dragon whose breath withers and
destroys the fleets of commerce — paralyzes the arm of industry — and arrays
every person against his neighbor," he wrote in 1891.[6] In Waite's estimation
monopoly was a nearly universal phenomenon, comprising "land monopoly,
money monopoly, transportation monopoly, trade monopoly, patent
monopoly, liquor monopoly and any or all other monopolies,"[7] all of which
enjoyed the protection of the "Associated Press monopoly, which alters or
suppresses all items of news as supposed best for the interests of monopoly."[8]
In fact, the various monopolies had converted the United States from a
republic into a "plutocratic oligarchy."[9]

Among the plethora of monopolies which afflicted America, Waite regarded land monopoly as the most vicious. Even the rudimentary idea of private
ownership of land — monopolistic or otherwise — was a travesty, or, as Waite
put it, "legalized robbery — the earth belongs to all the people in usufruct."[10]
Land monopoly, however, was the most pernicious manifestation of private
ownership of land and Waite dwelt often upon the theme. Yet he had little
use for the ideas of Henry George and ridiculed the idea that landowners
dominated the world. They were mere instruments of another monopoly, the
monopoly of money, and therefore the appropriate correctives for land monopoly had to be applied to the corporate level by chastising landed railroads
and land companies.[11] This recommended course of action was only an elabo-
ration of an idea in the Omaha Platform.

If anti-monopoly attitudes formed the functional part of Waite's reform
creed, the Omaha Platform of the People's Party was his Bible, his holy writ.
He accepted the Omaha document wholly, without reservation or equivoca-
tion. Its ideas and recommendations represented absolute truth, and all of
them were equal in importance. In consequence, Waite, a moral absolutist,
saw the world in terms of a cleavage between the robbers and the robbed. Private ownership of land and of railroads, for example, comprised "a charter
from the government to rob without fear of any laws."[12] Hence Waite held
relatively "advanced" views on such issues as land and public utilities, and
these aspects of his thought contradicted the old-fashioned Jeffersonianism of
his other attitudes.

As editor of the Aspen *Union Era* Waite advocated the entire stock of Populist principles. In and of itself the free coinage of silver was a decidedly secondary matter, though Waite was ultimately forced to revise his sense of
priorities in the face of political reality.[13] Reflecting the labor base of Colorado reformism, however, the demands which he emphasized most often were
lien law reform, the eight-hour day, the prohibition of child labor and the

control of Pinkerton detectives. But he reserved his most caustic broadsides and his best expletives for the one evil which underlay all others—the monopoly of money.[14]

"The abundance and scarcity of money are the great causes of national prosperity and decadence, and philosophically must be," Waite avowed, "and learning, civil and religious tolerance, and the rights of men are only adjuncts...."[15] Misery and social decay were products of a declining level of prices fostered by the partisans of a constricted money supply. This was not necessarily a plea for free silver, for Waite was closer to the Greenback position in his advocacy of a scientifically managed money supply. Waite became a silverite slowly and with reluctance, professing trepidation about his change of heart and concluding that Wall Street would retaliate against free silver by removing National Bank notes from circulation and thus counteract the expansive effect of silver.[16] Moreover, he could not accept the idea of silver as an inflationary device, knowing that inflation was just as likely to damage the position of wage-earning Colorado miners as deflation by wiping out gains in real wages.[17] "Money," said Waite in words reminiscent of William V. Allen, "is made by law," but his position as a silver state Populist forced him ultimately to profess that the money made by law should be silver money.[18]

In addition, Waite expressed the usual Populist contempt for the National Banking System and the Federal government's bonding policy, and he regarded controversy over the tariff component of national revenue policy as a contrived issue. The banking system was just another monopoly, a useless fraud, and private banking in general was a deliberate and malicious device to create an aristocracy of wealth by enabling the banker "to collect interest on what he owes."[19] Like Allen, Waite regarded the national debt and the issuance of bonds as another reprehensible manipulation of the money monopoly. *"Carthage delenda est,"* he announced on one occasion, "which may be freely translated as 'the bonding system must be destroyed.'"[20] But the tariff had no apparent relationship to monopoly or to anything else, and Waite considered free trade and protectionism as equally fallacious. After all, he argued, there was little reason to think that free trade would lower prices in the domestic market when the foreign suppliers were as likely to be monopolists as the American producers.[21]

Waite's writings in the *Union Era* made him well known in Colorado radical circles some time before his actual political career commenced. His trenchant advocacy of Populist doctrine was considered to be "able and fervent," and he projected himself well as a "crusader of impassioned ardor" in the quest for far-reaching social reform.[22] As a non-agrarian, Waite perhaps had a better view of the social process than most Populists, but his intellect and his perceptiveness were hardly distinguished and he assessed all of contemporary reality through the opaque glass of anti-monopoly.

The nomination and election in 1892 of Davis Waite as Populist governor of Colorado were the results of events as fortuitous as the experience of Lewelling in Kansas. While Lewelling was generally unknown, however, Waite's reputation was dubious. Many described him as an old crank (he was 68), and there was no doubt that he was bombastic, sharp-tongued, prone to malicious characterization of his opponents, and otherwise distinguished by the biblical and classical allusions which abounded in his outdated oratory.[23] Except for the words in which they were cast there was little uniqueness in his ideas. Among Populists there was considerable opposition to his nomination, for many party members regarded him as visionary or fanatic. Silver Democrats in Colorado, whose views were articulated by the *Rocky Mountain News* (Denver), denied him support that might have been useful. For his part, Waite spurned the Democratic silverites and later emerged as one of the most articulate critics of Democratic-Populist fusion.[24]

But the old man worked diligently, campaigning in nearly every county and frequently emphasizing the Populist pledge to reduce the salaries of public officials. Nevertheless, his election by the slender margin of 3,000 votes was primarily a reflection of his party's impeccable credentials on the silver policy issue.[25] Like his contemporary in Kansas, however, Waite was thwarted from the beginning by a legislature controlled by political adversaries, and though Colorado experienced no "legislative war," friction between Waite and the General Assembly was unending. Waite, in fact, provoked much of it himself. With the Assembly dominated by Republicans and the Senate controlled by Democrats and Populists who made no pretense of cooperation, the Waite administration was beaten at the start.[26]

For some unexplained reason, Waite dwelt upon railroad reform as the principal theme of his inaugural message. To the population of a state where plummeting silver prices threatened economic prostration this was politically inept. His other inaugural proposals—compulsory arbitration, the eight-hour day, a revised lien law, debt relief, employers' liability, the direct election of Senators and woman suffrage—were more congruous to the local political reality and demonstrated again the working-class orientation of mountain state Populism. In addition, Waite championed the abolition of capital punishment, the prohibition of convict labor on non-state projects, the creation of a state Board of Health, the establishment of a system of free kindergartens, and, lastly, the unlimited coinage of silver.[27]

Few of Waite's proposals were enacted into law, and these were ideologically innocuous suggestions like dairy inspection, the board of health, and free kindergartens.[28] Moreover, from the beginning of his two-year tenure Waite had such difficulties with appointed personnel that Lewelling's problems in Kansas seem minor by comparison. He admitted a tendency to appoint men with the "right views," and while these sycophants lent their official support to the governor they quietly secured entree to the state treasury or devised other extra-legal means of self-enrichment. In retrospect Waite admitted that he had "undoubtedly appointed more scalawags to office than any governor who ever lived."[29] Hence, in the course of one biennium, he felt obligated twice to dismiss two of the three members of the Denver Police and Fire Board for non-enforcement of the gambling laws, a member of the State Medical Board for unauthorized use of state funds, two members of the State Board of Agriculture for incompetence (or fraud) in the selection of education lands, the State Inspector of Coal Mines for neglect of safety standards, and three Penitentiary Commissioners for illegal appointments and parole practices.[30]

If any aspect of his internal administration necessitated continuous attention, it was the enforcement of the gambling laws and his "war" with the Denver gamblers and their supporters in the city government. Just as Lewelling had a fixation with prohibition enforcement, Waite's moral nature led him to extremes in the matter of gambling. Denver was an "open" city, and Waite vainly tried "to impose his ideals on a worldly and pleasure-loving community," sure of the righteousness of his convictions.[31] Yet his "war" on the gamblers exposed a purely legalistic side to his personality, and when hardpressed he retreated from moralism to legalism. He intended to close the "whisky saloons and gambling houses" at the appropriate times, he wrote in a memorandum of 1894 to the agents of enforcement, "not because of the outcries of the Doctors of Divinity ... the Women's Christian Temperance Union or the prohibitionists ... but because it is a duty imposed upon us by the law."[32] The windmill at which he tilted continued to stand, and, perhaps illustrative of his moral norms, he devoted most of the first issue of his postgubernatorial mouthpiece *Waite's Magazine* to Denver gambling and to his "war" on the gamblers.[33] There was more to this than politics, however, for Waite believed that "Christians" were the most likely to be addicted to gambling and to surpass professed Christians in the context of their own moral precepts was for him a perpetual compulsion.

But Waite was not without his personal contradictions. In spite of the near-socialism of some of his views, Waite did not advocate an expansion of state services so far as security and welfare were concerned. Social services involved expenditures, and it was Waite's belief that state funds might best remain unspent. This was characteristic of the parsimony common among

Populists and so well illustrated by their abhorrence of debt. Waite called for the strictest economy in government. Even with increased law enforcement costs occasioned by labor conflict in the mines and his own battle with the city administration of Denver, the Waite administration's expenditures were fifteen percent less than those of the preceding Republican administration.[34] Admittedly, part of this may have been due to Waite's inability to control his own party in the legislature and to the collateral fact that only eleven of his seventy-eight legislative proposals were enacted. Where expenditures were not involved or where humanity actually resulted in lessened costs Waite acted with dispatch, however. In the course of his tenure as governor he reduced the burden on the state prison system to the extent of 113 pardons and 22 commutations.[35]

Rebuked by the legislature in its regular session, Waite concluded that prudence dictated a special session. "We stand," he alleged, "upon the brink of industrial slavery."[36] His particular solution to the problems of depression, unemployment and deprivation in 1894 was to suspend the laws which brought down the heavy hand of the state on rural and urban debtors unable to meet their obligations. He did not suggest, or even consider, committing the resources of the state to provide positive assistance to the unemployed and the poor.[37] While tax and debt relief undoubtedly kept some funds from reaching the coffers of the state it did not necessarily follow that the funds were retained by the poor for their own use since the poor ordinarily failed to receive the income in the first place.

If the Waite administration was unwilling to put the positive resources of the state at the disposal of the needy, the image of the administration was also damaged by the inflammatory and idiosyncratic character of Waite himself. On a podium he thrived on the response of audiences and his utterances were more extreme than his intentions. Enemies regarded him as a madman, and he often played into their hands. Three events of national prominence stand out as illustrative of his penchant, perhaps a bit playful, for effect: his notorious "bloody bridles" address, his espousal of the "fandango" dollar scheme, and his role in the Cripple Creek strike of 1894.

In an address delivered on July 11, 1893, to a crowd at the Denver Coliseum assembled to protest the Cleveland administration's proposal to repeal the Sherman Silver Purchase Law — a repeal action which ultimately did force silver prices down to the point that many Colorado mines were closed as uneconomic enterprises and which did devastate the mining areas — Waite, in a carefully prepared speech, made some popular and telling points. He argued that repeal was a manifestation of the "goldbug" conspiracy to promote deflation in order to increase the value of money expressed in bonds and mortgages. He declared that Cleveland's behavior on the issue of Sherman Act repeal was the most reprehensible action "since Louis XIV revoked the Edict of Nantes." But he added that in the struggle against exploitation by the plutocracy "our weapons are argument and the ballot — a free ballot and a fair count." But if suppression by the plutocracy should reach the point where hostility and social upheaval were necessary, then so be it, he declared, "for it is better, infinitely better, that blood should flow to the horses' bridles than our national liberties should be destroyed."[38] This paraphrase of *Revelation* 14:20, which confirmed Waite's reputation as a revolutionary, was mainly a reflection of his oratorical predilection for biblical analogies.

Perhaps of greater meaning and consequence was Waite's advocacy of the Mexican silver dollar or "fandango" dollar plan which he devised to mitigate the effects of the Sherman repeal and the economic catastrophe it provoked in Colorado. This was more than a monetary expedient, for it also demonstrated that Waite's political attitudes were cast in the same state sovereignty mold that characterized his contemporary in Kansas. In this sense, at least, Waite was something of an old Jeffersonian.

The "fandango" dollar scheme was a plan to ship Colorado silver to Mexico, secure its coinage into Mexican dollars, pay the seignorage to the Mexican government, and transport the coins back to Colorado for use as legal tender within the state. Waite carried on a brief correspondence with Mexican president Porfirio Diaz about his plan and viewed the results as encouraging.[39] While the "fandango" dollar idea, incredible but not original in itself,[40] has ordinarily been thought of as an inflationary device, it was also an idea rooted in a particular and distinct conception of the essence of the American Union. Whether it was a crack-brained scheme or not was beside the point.

Waite explained the basis of his proposal to the Colorado legislature and to the general public in the *North American Review*. The constitutional power of Congress to coin money and to regulate its value, he contended, was an "exclusive" right only so long as it was "exercised," and Congress had refused to exercise the right so far as silver was concerned after the Sherman Silver Act repeal of October, 1893.[41] Constitutionally, individual states possessed the power to make (or keep) gold and silver coins legal tender, for only the pre-constitutional right to emit bills of credit had been surrendered by the states by the terms of constitutional ratification. Hence the right "to coin money, regulate the value thereof and of foreign coins" could not be arbitrarily exercised by Congress. Moreover, since foreign coins circulated in the United States at the time the Constitution was drafted and ratified, and since their continued circulation was implied in the text of the document, the Federal law of 1857 which proscribed foreign coins was clearly unconstitutional, for congressional power extended only to the determination of the value of foreign coins and not to the fact of their circulation. Waite cited the appropriate authorities—Albert Gallatin, Daniel Webster and Thomas Hart Benton—to lend substance to his claim that the 1857 law was invalid.[42]

More basic, however, were the constitutional assumptions which underlay this projected re-entry of the States into the monetary field. Waite designated as "axioms" that all rights possessed by Congress were concessions from the States and that no right possessed by a state derived from the Constitution. Since the states preceded the Constitution the rights of states were naturally preexistent and inviolate. Even if these assumptions were not granted, Waite alleged, the right of states to employ foreign and domestic coins was, by guarantee of the Constitution itself, "a concurrent and independent right ... and may be exercised and operative within the boundaries of the State entirely independent of any action of Congress."[43] It would be difficult, if not impossible, to find a better expression of strict-construction doctrine in the late nineteenth century.

Similarly, Waite condemned the deployment of Federal troops and marshals in Colorado during the Pullman strike in the summer of 1894 on the exclusive grounds of state sovereignty doctrine. He adamantly contended that the Federal presence constituted a violation of Article IV Section 4 of the Constitution, which guaranteed to every state freedom from invasion and a republican form of government. He further alleged that the rights of a "sovereign state" had been transgressed by "Presidential usurpation," and, to compound the travesty, "judicial usurpation" in violation of Article II Section 3 and the Fourth, Fifth, and Sixth amendments also occurred when Federal marshals, operating under the authority of Federal judicial decrees, seized county courthouses and used them as recruiting stations for deputies who interfered with the legal activities of Colorado citizens. These sentiments. of course, were paralleled in Kansas by Governor Lewelling.

Finally, Waite's personal intervention on the side of striking miners at Cripple Creek in 1894, his use of state military power to offset the power of management and to protect the strikers, and his advocacy of the miners' cause even to the point of wearing the white armband of the strikers may have been unique, but it was consistent with his philosophy and with political reality. Miners, after all, had put him in office, and to have assumed a position of neutrality in the strike would have made him an ally of the plutocrats, negating the entire meaning of his governorship. Those who expressed surprise because the "state military has never before been used in defense of the rights of labor" demonstrated more comprehension of the Colorado social structure than understanding of Davis Waite.[44]

Given the circumstances of his election, the pattern of his behavior, and the structural weakness of the People's Party in Colorado, there was little doubt but that Waite would be a one-term governor, an incongruity in the state's political history. Colorado Populism was so tenuous, and so splintered, that by 1894 three rival People's Party organizations were active in some parts of the state. Waite, however, would not believe that he was only a historical peculiarity. After his resounding defeat in 1894, for instance, he told the newly assembled and Republican-dominated legislature in his final message: "We go, but we return. We will meet you, gentlemen, in two years, at Philippi."[45]

Following his departure from public life Waite tried to play a larger role in the deliberations and proceedings of the national Populist party. The Omaha Platform still lived, and Waite watched with dismay as the party leaders moved toward fusion with the Democracy. He became a prominent member of the middle-of-the-road faction in the party, a faction which opposed the single-minded attraction of the party to free silver and which earned the designation by the National Chairman of the party as a little group of "cranks and socialists."[46] But by 1896 Waite was in search of a discreet compromise, and to his later regret he ultimately accepted the Bryan candidacy. At home, however, he led a rump middle-of-the-road faction against the Fusionists in 1896, and he received a gubernatorial vote so small that, in total, it hardly exceeded his 3,000 vote margin of victory in 1892.[47]

Perhaps because of his age, time did little to change Waite's mind about the direction and structure of American life. He ended the 1890s as he had begun the decade, obsessed with the omnipresence of monopoly. Like another fallen hero, Jerry Simpson, Waite felt obligated to create his own periodical in order to continue dissemination of his message, but *Waite's Magazine* (1898) suspended publication after two issues, leaving him without a vehicle for his ideas.[48] Though he could write in 1898 that "monopoly of a public nature, organized in the interest of caste ... is sucking the lifeblood of the prosperity and liberty of the nation,"[49] his anti-monopoly attitudes softened. His disgust at the direction of his party, a party which had been "sold out by traitors like Weaver and Butler,"[50] may have wrenched him free from his dogmatism. In any event, by the middle of 1897 he interested himself in a colony scheme in Texas, an enterprise which brought him into contact with "some of the biggest landholders in the state of Texas"[51] and failed to tap his reservoir of animus for land monopoly. And in 1898 he told his dwindling band of middle-of-the-road followers to vote Republican in the Colorado governorship contest, alleging that the Republican candidate was less dishonorable than the fusionist Democrat.[52]

The Spanish-American War and the related question of empire provided the final crisis of faith and spirit for Davis Waite. Witnessing the growing body of Democrats in the anti°imperialist camp and the emergence of Bryan as a foe of empire, Waite's denouement was completed. "I am as good a Republican as anyone," he avowed in 1900. "I never had any use for a Democrat anyway. They are just the same way now that they were during our war with the South; they were against the government then and secretly sympathized with our enemy."[53] Though he lived another five years, Waite's public career ended with those words.

In his relationship to the Populist movement in Colorado, Waite sided with the miners and other wage laborers, and he was thus on the left wing of the movement. The agrarian right wing of the party usually opposed him. Yet his position on the left was never unequivocal, for he was unwilling to commit resources in a positive manner to mitigate the effects of unemployment and social dislocation. While he did not advocate the restoration of pure competition as a cure for monopoly, he could not extricate his ideas from negativism. He emphasized class-conflict without any connection with Marxism, and at the same time apparently believed in a (John C.) Calhoun-like conception of the national polity. There may have been no contradiction here, however. Just as Calhoun could view slavery as a paternal institution and analyze social processes in such a class conscious manner that Richard Hofstadter called him the "Marx of the Master Class,"[54] Waite could also view society in terms of class conflict and then allege, as he did in 1898, that "the greatest evidence of progress in modern civilization is the tendency of civil government to paternalism."[55] Perhaps this was the order of progress in nineteenth century America—from paternal slaveholder to paternal bureaucrat. The idea evoked scorn from other Populists.

If Waite had a slight ideological connection with the Jeffersonian tradition, however, he had no relationship to the Jeffersonian performance over the entirety of the nineteenth century. While the party of Jefferson made a home for immigrants and took ethnic minorities to its bosom, Waite was a thoroughgoing nativist, hostile to the existence of the Indians and the Spanish-speaking in Colorado and opposed to the Chinese and to the "new immigration."[56] On balance, he had one of the least original minds in the Populist movement. Swearing allegiance to the Omaha Platform was an experience akin to religious conversion, and in the functional phase of his career he was unable to think outside of its context. Over time he was sustained primarily by his obsession with monopoly, by his evangelical moral fervor, and by his compulsion to introduce morality into the public service such as did not exist in the "Godless, nominally Christian"[57] governments which functioned around him in order to placate his personal God of righteousness.

COLLECTIVITIES

CHAPTER SIX

Populism in the State Legislatures:
An Analysis of Seven Western States

One useful and fundamental key to the ambivalent but essentially conservative nature of the Populist movement is afforded by examining the legislative performance of Populists in the legislatures of states dominated or markedly influenced by the movement. This poses a cruel paradox and reveals an unfortunate contradiction in Populism, for, if it is assumed that the 1892 Omaha Platform of the People's Party accurately mirrored the substantive concerns and priorities of the party's adherents, then Populism, by making its most significant inroads into the domain of ordinary two-party politics at the level of state government, thereby insured its own impotence.[1] Populism's basic involvement with issues of land, transportation and money meant that at the level of state government, where Populists acquired the most power to induce change, they also had the least authority to effect it. Of the three areas of crucial significance to the party, only the area of land policy lay within its province at the state level and then only in a marginal way, since all Populist states contained large blocs of public domain which were effectively outside of state authority. Nevertheless, Populist legislative performance in the states offers substantial illustration of the constricted, special interest nature of the movement.

In this analysis, the composition and behavior of Populist legislators in western states which experienced a substantial Populist intrusion into the normal political pattern were studied in the contexts of the legislatures of 1891, 1893 and 1897, with ancillary attention devoted to 1895, a year in which Populist fortunes ebbed considerably. The states were Kansas, Nebraska, South Dakota, Idaho, Montana, Colorado and Washington. In these states more than 20,000 legislative bills were introduced in the 1891-1897 period, only a small proportion of which possessed "reform" characteristics and only a fraction of these were ever brought to a vote. Yet a critical scrutiny of this raw legislative material proved instructive and enlightening.

Serious conceptual problems occur with this kind of analysis, however, and the nature of these problems requires detailed explanation. The root assumption, of course, was that Populists would be more inclined to sponsor and support reform proposals consistent with the party's rhetoric and platform than members of the other parties. Unfortunately, it was not always possible to distinguish Populists from non-Populists with precision, for party designations were by no means clear in all cases. Especially in the 1897 sessions, following the fusion of the Populists and Bryanite Democrats, confused and imprecise party designations—Silver Republican, Populist-Democrat, Democrat-Populist— occurred with considerable frequency. In spite of this irremediable obfuscation, meaningful questions could still be put to the legislatures of these states. What kind of "reform" legislation did Populists sponsor? Did Populists generally support the legislative efforts of their colleagues? Did Populists introduce more, or less, reform legislation than their proportional strength in a legislative body would seem to warrant? Did members of the established parties support or reject Populist-sponsored bills? Did Populists behave as reformers on a relatively broad base or only in a limited, special-interest context? This last question was gauged to discern whether Populists were really committed social critics or merely reflective of the disenchantment of one or more narrowly structured interest groups.

These queries, in turn, raised a serious question of method. What was "reform" legislation? To supply an answer to this question, especially given the profusion of bills and memorials perennially considered within state legislative bodies, it was necessary to make some arbitrary inclusions and some equally arbitrary exclusions of matters which sometimes contained genuine ingredients of ideological conflict. Thus, for the purposes delineated here, "reform" legislation was defined in part by ascertaining what it was not as well as what it was. Excluded were such issues as the regulation of telephone companies, a matter of largely urban concern in the 1890s, and legislation pertaining to matters of personal morality and familial relationships—marriage, divorce, gambling, alcoholic beverages, child custody, minors and orphans. Municipal charter reform, the regulation of insurance companies, amendments to existing portions of criminal or civil codes, and the woman suffrage question were also excluded because Populists never attempted to make these issues Populist issues in a partisan sense. On the other hand, the following kinds of legislative proposals were considered to be genuinely Populist and worth analysis: railroad bills of various kinds, especially those which dealt with freight rate regulation, passenger fares, liability for injury and damage, and the creation or improvement of regulatory commissions; land reform proposals, particularly limitations on alien or absentee land ownership; attempts to revise or control the legal rate of interest; petitions, memorials and legislation relative to legal tender and the coinage of silver; tax relief; liberalization of mortgage foreclosure and redemption procedures for agricultural real estate; regulatory legislation regarding the operation of stockyards and grain storage facilities; reform of banking practices, especially by means of the creation of banking commissions; anti-trust and anti-monopoly bills; labor legislation, particularly wages, hours, and working conditions proposals, the proscription of Pinkerton detectives and imported militia in labor disputes, and mine safety; state tax reform; and adjustments in electoral procedure such as the Australian ballot.

In considering the input and output of legislatures either dominated or markedly influenced by the Populists several points emerged with clarity. In the first place, Populist legislators, with the sole exception of railroad matters, were *not demonstrably* more likely to introduce major reform proposals than members of the other parties, and in some instances they were even less likely to do so. Secondly, and again with the exception of railroad measures, Populists were not more inclined to support reform proposals in the plains states than were members of the established parties, but they were distinctly more inclined toward reform than were the other parties in the mining states. This fact alone suggests that considerable ideological division existed in the movement between its agrarian and laborite factions, although this conclusion may be indicative only of differentiated regional rather than occupational conditions. But considerable evidence to corroborate the view that labor-based mining state Populism was more reformist than agrarian-oriented prairie state Populism is afforded by the example of Nebraska, a pre-eminent Populist state, where Republicans in the state legislature were often more congenial to reform than the Democrats and where, in the long run, Populists were able to collaborate and ultimately coalesce with the Democrats. It is an accurate generalization, nevertheless, that Populists in many states did not sponsor or sustain reform legislation to a measurably greater extent than their competitors on the basis of a strict proportional comparison within the various legislative bodies. On the other hand, it seems to be equally true that the presence of Populists in state legislatures had a certain "softening" effect on the attitudes of the other parties and helped to galvanize latent reform propensities within the major parties. This, of course, is consistent with the usual interpretation of the functional role of third-parties in the United States.

Moreover, the locus of Populist interests varied substantively between the plains and mountain regions and represented the differentiated regional constituencies within the party. In the plains area the bulk of reform proposals impinged upon agriculture and the commercial institutions utilized by farmers in the marketing process, namely railroad facilities, storage elevators and stockyards. Yet considerable labor legislation was also introduced in the prairie states, surely more of it than the wage laborer interests of these states warranted. Populist legislation in the Mountain region, on the other hand, was almost exclusively concerned with labor conditions and with memorials and petitions to Congress on the silver coinage issue. Colorado and Washington comprised a partial exception to this generalization and exhibited an agrarian-labor mix of approximately equal proportions.

Even more important than the farmer-labor dichotomy, however, was the realization that little Populist-sponsored legislation, except for railroad bills, triggered markedly partisan responses. Populist bills which passed one or both houses of a legislature were ordinarily approved overwhelmingly and did not seem to activate ideological sensitivities. That Populists in general differed little from members of the other parties in terms of most socio-economic variables has been amply demonstrated in the case of Kansas by Walter T. K. Nugent and O. Gene Clanton, and it may be fairly presumed that no serious student any longer accepts the old charges that Populists were madmen or political psychopaths.[2] Hence, an examination of Populist legislative behavior provides confirmation for the view that the principal basis for the vitriolic anti-Populist rhetoric indulged in by Republicans and others in the 1890s was just that—rhetoric. Indeed, some of the most trenchant opposition to Populist legislative measures came from factions *within* the party rather than from Republicans or Democrats.[3] Considered collectively, moreover, Populist state legislators presented an image of negligible discipline, substantial internal contradiction and marked ambivalence, and the total output of Populist reform legislation was hardly commensurate with the critical energies and ideological panic engendered by the third-party phenomenon. Populist state legislators were remarkably adept at disposing of their own proposals by defeating them in the legislative bodies in which they originated.

Turning to the Populist-dominated or influenced legislatures themselves, the veracity of these contentions may be illustrated and refined. In consequence of the major Populist victory in 1896 in Kansas, the governorship and both houses of the state legislature came under Populist control. At no other time and in no other state did the party succeed as completely in capturing the administrative and legislative apparatus of a state, and, without effective opposition, it might have been expected that the Kansas legislative session of 1897 would be productive and reformist. But nothing could be further from the truth. The session did not lack for proposals, for the legislative houses entertained more than 1500 bills.[4] Of these, not more than ten (less duplications) bore on matters of fundamental concern to Populism as described in the principal statements of the party's creed, and, peculiarly, many of the reform bills dealt with labor problems—the demand for weekly remuneration, protection of the rights of individuals who affiliated with labor unions, relief of unemployed wage earners, and the prohibition of blacklisting.[5] Other reformist measures included an anti-trust bill, a warehouse regulation proposal, a stockyards bill (a perennial in Kansas and Nebraska legislatures), an agricultural laborer's lien bill, an interest rate bill, and a maximum passenger fare bill for the state's railroads.[6] Only one of these, the stockyards regulation proposal, came to a vote, and it failed.[7] Most of the other reform measures failed to clear the Populist-dominated committees of the respective legislative houses.

The principal Populist achievement of the 1897 Kansas legislature was the passage of a bill to establish by law maximum rates for the transportation of freight by rail. Railroad regulation, of course, was the preeminent Populist issue in the plains region, but it was an issue as divisive within as without the Populist coalition.[8] In simplest terms the issue involved not the necessity of regulation but the most effective means to achieve it. In Populist circles one faction, generally coincident with the intransigent "middle-of-the-road" group who scorned cooperation with the other parties, tended to favor the establishment of maximum rates by statute, while the more cooperative and moderate "fusionist" group, which often coalesced with the Democrats, inclined toward vesting the rate-making authority in a state commission either created or restructured for this purpose. The leaders of Kansas Populism in 1897 had endorsed and benefited from fusion, and the Populist governor, John W. Leedy, was known to favor the commission approach.[9] But the Populist controlled legislature, with only one dissenting vote, passed a maximum-rate bill and ultimately enacted it by overriding the governor's veto.[10]

Political motives in the Kansas railroad reform imbroglio were obviously complex. Republican legislators saw the bill as a short-run mechanism to embarrass the administration and doubtless realized that, in the long run, an altered legislative composition might adjust the maximum rates to make them acceptable to any particular constituency. Middle-of-the-road Populists regarded the maximum-rate bill as an expression of direct democracy, and by the exertion of considerable pressure upon their fusionist colleagues induced them to contravene the administration position. Subsequently, by formal declaration, forty-four legislators admitted their belief that the legislation in which they had acquiesced contravened the best interests of the state.[11]

Farmer's Alliance and People's party members comprised a substantial proportion of Kansas legislators from 1891 through 1897, and, like so many insurgent states, Kansas experienced its most active reform legislature in 1891, when the political upheaval of the 1890s was still in an informal and relatively spontaneous phase. The Kansas legislature of 1891 consisted of a Farmer's

Alliance-Populist controlled House, the members of which were elected in 1890, and a Republican dominated Senate, largely consisting of holdovers from the previous session.[12] In the course of the session the legislature enacted a law restricting alien ownership of land in Kansas, a law establishing an eight-hour day for laborers on state and municipal projects, a law regulating warehouses and the inspection, weighing and handling of grain, and a law prohibiting combinations in the state's livestock trade.[13] The same legislature quashed an attempt to establish maximum railroad rates, a bill to establish a board of railroad commissioners, a child labor measure, and a bill to regulate the legal rate of interest.[14] *Every* successful measure in the 1891 legislature originated in the Republican Senate and with Republican sponsorship. Every unsuccessful reform bill in the same session derived from the Alliance-Populist House, and, with the exception of two railroad bills which died in Senate committees and a measure to reform coal-weighing procedures in the state's mines, the reforms proposed in the House failed to clear the legislative body in which they originated.[15] Owing to the "Legislative War" of 1893, which pitted rival Populist and Republican lower houses against each other for much of the session, the legislature of that year was a reform disaster. And, in 1895, Populist fortunes in Kansas reached their lowest point and productive legislation favorable to the Populists failed to materialize.[16] On the basis of performance criteria, therefore, the affirmation that Kansas comprised the heartland of Populist sentiment was less than impressive.

Indeed, if any state merited the reputation for Populist preeminence, as determined by a sustained and longlived reformist thrust, that state was Nebraska. Unfortunately, Nebraska Populists controlled the legislature but not the governorship in 1891, neither the executive nor the legislature in 1893, and the governorship but not the legislature in 1895, 1897 and 1899.[17] While the inconsistency explicit in this pattern of electoral success may appear peculiar at first glance, it is in reality a constituent element of a larger problem, posed in question form in one way or another by several recent scholars, the question being "Who were the Nebraska Populists?"[18] A satisfactory answer to this elementary question has not yet been forthcoming, for the sources of Populist support among the Nebraska voters seemed to be tenuous and continually in flux. Serious hypotheses and well-conceived studies of sample counties and precincts designed to isolate the sources of Populist strength have yielded diverse and incompatible conclusions. Nebraska's rural Populists, like their compatriots in Kansas, do not seem to have been drawn mainly from the ranks of depression-vulnerable wheat farmers.[19] Nor, contrary to one notable hypothesis, did Nebraska Populism reflect a temporary alliance of farmers and village merchants. The Populist urban vote increased considerably in 1892,[20] but this urban vote was more than offset by the attrition of rural voters for Populist strength in the state legislature decreased by more than twenty percent as a result of the 1892 elections.[21] And the 1893 legislature, which presumably reflected an urban shift in Nebraska Populist strength, afforded no evidence of increased emphasis on reform concerns of interest to city or village dwellers. Then, in 1894, the full impact of the depression which commenced in 1893 turned Nebraska voters further away from the alleged reformers and dissidents and back into their traditional Republican voting patterns.[22]

Nevertheless, Nebraska Populists were the most broadly and consistently reformist group within the movement. Independents, i.e. Populists, composed 54% of the Nebraska legislature in 1891, 40% in 1893, 23% in 1895 and nearly 50% in 1897.[23] But in Nebraska, as in Kansas, Populists were really no more likely to sponsor or support reform measures than members of the established parties, and the role of Populism seemed to be to create a symbiotic relationship with the other parties pursuant to which some reform legislation was enacted. For example, Independents (Populists) in the 1891 legislature sponsored nine of twenty-one (42%) of the reform bills in the House while comprising 54% of its membership, and one of five reform proposals (20%) in the Senate, though comprising 52% of that body.[24] Republicans, who represented 21% of the House membership and 20% of the Senate, sponsored eight (40%) of the reform bills in the former body and two (40%) in the latter.[25]

Populist legislation in the 1891 Nebraska legislature included two railroad bills, a liberal mortgage foreclosure bill, a bill to forbid foreign individuals and corporations from speculating in Nebraska lands, a stockyards control measure, drought relief, an interest rate bill, and a bill to prohibit free passes on railroads in the state.[26] On the other hand, Republicans or Democrats proposed measures to deal with speculation in the commodities markets, a bill to suspend the collection of delinquent taxes, an eight-hour day bill, employers' liability, electoral reforms, anti-trust legislation, a mechanic's lien bill, a bill forbidding "yellow dog" contracts, and bills regulating warehouses, mines, and farm mortgages, and railroad rate regulation.[27] It is obvious that the sphere of reform interests of Populists was distinctly narrower than that of reformers in the other parties. Only two of these bills passed the legislature, and only one, the drought relief bill, was signed by the governor.[28] The other, a comprehensive Populist railroad measure, elicited a gubernatorial veto which was sustained by a close vote in the Senate.[29]

Nebraska legislatures with a minority contingent of Populists were in fact more productive of reform legislation than the insurgent dominated session of

1891. Again this demonstrated that successful reform legislation was largely a function of Republican-Populist concord. Nebraska provided a distinctive example of the ambivalent pattern of prairie populism — a successful insurgency in 1890 followed by legislative disappointment in 1891, electoral reverses of modest proportions in 1892 followed by a *more* successful reform output in the 1893 session, an electoral debacle in 1894 accompanied by reform atrophy in 1895, electoral recovery in 1896 succeeded by an 1897 session of negligible productivity. On balance, it appears that the role of Populism was to soften Republican resistance to reform and that the key to successful reform legislation lay as much in Republican behavior as in Populist leadership.

The 1893 Nebraska legislature, for example, had a Populist representation of 40% in the House and 39% in the Senate. Twenty-three reform bills were introduced into the House, eleven (45%) of them by Populists, while five of eight (65%) of reform proposals in the Senate were Populist sponsored.[30] Populist reform interests seemed to broaden as the party's legislative strength diminished, for Populists in 1893 offered bills dealing with Pinkerton detectives, railroad rates and railroad liability for personal injury, drought relief, protection of members of labor unions, weekly wages, the adulteration of food and drugs, legal tender currency and futures speculation in the commodities markets.[31] Only the railroad bills and drought relief were enacted, but Republicans and/or Democrats sponsored and passed a price-fixing prohibition, a stockyards control bill, and a bill to outlaw sweatshop labor.[32]

Nebraska's 1895 session was less instructive. Populists experienced severe electoral reverses in 1894 and comprised less than 25% of the 1895 legislature. Reform proposals were fewer — fourteen in all — and only four of them were of Populist sponsorship.[33] None of the Populist bills passed the legislature, and Nebraska Populists, who had a sympathetic governor for the first time in 1895, seemed to have run out of ideas. The only successful reform emanating from the session was the creation of a State Banking Board and a bank examiner system, a Republican measure endorsed overwhelmingly by all parties in the legislature.[34]

In 1896 Nebraska Populism, benefiting from Populist-Democratic fusion in national politics and from the endorsement of a native son, William Jennings Bryan, as standard bearer for both parties, reemerged as a potent political force. The 1897 legislative session was nearly 50% Populist in composition, and the party's members clearly dominated the legislature. A considerable number of reform proposals were put forward, including many of the old stand-bys — anti-trust legislation, railroad bills, stockyards regulation, revision of mortgage foreclosure procedures, corrupt practices bills, tax reform, employers' liability, and anti-blacklisting.[35] Despite a Populist plurality in the legislature and a Populist in the statehouse, the only major legislation enacted was a Republican measure to prevent combination in the grain elevator business and Populist corrupt practices and stockyards bills.[36] Some genuine reforms, such as an Australian ballot bill, an anti-trust bill and a measure extending the powers of the state's Board of Transportation, cleared the legislature but were not acted upon by the Populist governor.[37] The bills which did become law had been overwhelmingly approved by all parties, testifying again to the non-partisan nature of much "reform"legislation.[38] Hence, if Nebraska Populism proved anything, it was that the Populist role was catalytic, or stimulative, rather than dramatically creative. Populists spurred the reform process, but they hardly dominated it.

In Nebraska, as in other western states, Populists left a legacy of budgetary retrenchment and fiscal restraint. This was primarily the work of Governors Silas A. Holcomb (1895-1899), a fusionist, and William A. Poynter (1899-1901), a Populist, both of whom successfully promoted the retrenchment cause with legislatures which they did not otherwise dominate. Holcomb's administration, despite depressed conditions and declining revenues in his first term, attacked the state's indebtedness with the vigor characteristic of bond-hating Populists. In the course of four years the bonded indebtedness of Nebraska declined by more than $400,000 and the outstanding general fund warrants were cut by more than $350,000. Poynter, who succeeded Holcomb in 1899, presided over the liquidation of the state debt and bequeathed to his successor a handsome surplus after serving a single term in the governor's chair. Both Holcomb and Poynter secured the revenue surpluses necessary to reduce and eventually eliminate the debt by reducing ordinary state services and thoroughly pruning appropriations for prisons, geriatric institutions and soldiers' homes. To demonstrate the successful nature of these cutbacks, the Poynter administration prepared an elaborate table showing the reduced costs of institutional maintenance on a per-inmate basis.[39]

Populism in other prairie states was merely a pallid imitation of the Kansas and Nebraska experiences. South Dakota, for example, was a state which entered the Union as recently as 1889 but which nevertheless possessed a tradition of agrarian dissidence which dated from 1884 and the establishment of the first "farmer's club" by Henry Langford Loucks, a militant reformer and recent immigrant from Canada. The farmer's clubs were able to exert sufficient pressure upon the territorial legislature to secure an elevator and warehouse law in 1887, but the transformation of the clubs into an Independent Party in 1890 was not accompanied by further successes except for the election, in alliance with the Democrats, of James H. Kyle of Aberdeen to the United States Senate. In 1890 and 1892 the Independents (Populists) fared poorly in state elections, but the party did manage to secure the election of twenty-four Populists to the state legislature in 1894. Populists attained power in the state in 1896 only by forging a coalition with Democrats and dissident Silver Republicans, gaining a seventeen vote majority in the legislature and securing the election of Andrew Lee, a fusionist, to the governorship.[40]

The South Dakota legislature of 1897, following the fusionist triumph, was a reformer's fiasco. Populists spent much of the 1897 session investigating the conduct of previous administrations and achieved little. Yet more than 600 bills engaged the attention of the legislature, but only ten of them contained any reform content. Four railroad bills were introduced in the House, including the commonplace rate regulation, regulatory commission, and anti-free pass measures, and a House Populist offered a wage lien bill for agricultural laborers.[41] None of these reforms elicited any enthusiasm or support, but the Senate contributed a successful railroad measure of its own and a vague anti-monopoly bill which ultimately received the governor's signature.[42] The legislature also succeeded in establishing the principle of the secret ballot.[43] But again the successful bills passed almost without dissent. The railroad bill, for example, inspired one negative vote in the House and none in the Senate.[44]

Therefore, *at least* in the plains states, it is difficult to find any meaningful ideological conflict between Populists and the leadership of the established parties. It might be surmised that matters of patronage and power were more productive of conflict than differing assessments of the needs of the body politic, and the internal struggles which occurred within the People's Party over patronage and legislative prerogative in the few instances in which the party acquired power tend to confirm this suspicion.[45] In any event, when legislative behavior is employed as the criterion, the ideological differentiation between Populists and others was marginal in spite of the mutual recriminations inspired by the movement.

The Populist experience in the Rocky Mountain mining states differed considerably from that in the plains region. Mountain state Populism, with the exception of agrarian elements in Colorado and Washington, was almost entirely predicated upon the interests of wage laborers, particularly mine workers, though the People's party of Idaho attracted some mine operators because of its position on the silver issue.[46] Even the free coinage of silver, an issue which conceptually linked the Populists of the plains states with those of the mining regions, had a different rationale in both regions. On the plains silver represented an acceptable inflationary device to the dissident agrarians, while in the mountain states free silver was a matter of continued employment and profits. Divisive as an issue on the plains, the silver question possessed basic unifying characteristics in the mining states though this fact was obscured by the great miners strikes of 1894 in Idaho and Colorado. Moreover, the common dependence on silver and the strength of silver interests in all parties in the mountain region probably muted the thrust of Populism and retarded the insurgency in its earlier phases. There was no great dissident upsurge in 1890, for example, and with the exception of Colorado in 1892, the few successes of mountain state Populists derived from coalition efforts with the Democrats and, to a lesser extent, the Silver Republicans of 1896.[47]

The transition from agricultural to mining state Populism was most evident in Colorado. Davis Hanson Waite, as governor in 1893 and 1894, conducted himself with sufficient flamboyancy to obscure the deep divisions in the Colorado party between the more conservative agrarian interests and the radical mining faction. Unfortunately the Populist leaders in Colorado were neither miners nor farmers but came from mercantile, real estate and professional backgrounds and from the urban trades of Denver and the smaller cities. Hence the Colorado People's Party reflected not only tension between miners and farmers but also revealed a basic dichotomy between the leaders and the led. Though the leaders frequently possessed previous political experience, they had exhibited no propensity for third-party activism and their subsequent careers as reformers were generally attenuated. The Populists, pledging themselves to promote a mild reform program consisting of the eight-hour day principle, reduction of the salaries of state officials, and the free coinage of silver, carried the major state offices in the election of 1892 and comprised 42% of the House and 37% of the Senate in the 1893 and 1894 legislative sessions. Their legislative productivity, however, was almost negligible.[48]

Colorado's Populist legislators were undoubtedly an acute disappointment to Waite. Not only did they fail to generate any reform momentum, but they failed to bring most bills further than a first reading. Railroad regulation, an anti-wage garnishment bill, hours and wages proposals, a public employment office measure, and related labor legislation all failed to clear the relevant committees.[49] Aside from memorials to Congress asserting the need for an income tax and the free coinage of silver, the legislature managed only to amend the state's mechanic's lien law and to establish, perhaps illegally, the principle of silver as legal tender.[50]

The 1894 special session, convened primarily to rectify the dismal record of 1893, achieved even less. The Senate declined to initiate bills, and the House session revealed a cleavage between farmers and laborers which paralyzed the party. A bill to regulate maximum hours of labor, for example, was sabotaged by the agrarians, while the labor contingent counter-attacked by tabling an interest rate measure.[51] For all of the commentary and panic which Populism evoked in Colorado, its concrete challenge to the state's establishment was literally non-existent.

Just as Kansas acquired a reputation as the preeminent Populist state on the plains when in reality Nebraska deserved the plaudits, so Colorado and its flamboyant governor dominated mountain state Populism and obscured the fact that the insurgency in Idaho was more substantial and of longer duration. The People's Party of Idaho, organized in the spring of 1892, was dominated throughout its history by militant laborite elements drawn from the state's mining industry. Agrarians were a distinct minority in the party apparatus, though many of the early electoral successes of the party occurred in farming areas. But laborites dictated policy for the state's Populists, and even their commonplace involvement with railroad regulation demonstrated more concern with passenger than with freight rates.[52] But the essence of Idaho Populism consisted of agitation for silver coinage and the pressing interest of miners in wages, hours, working conditions, mine inspection, and tax relief for debtors and the unemployed. Populists in significant numbers (17% of the legislature) first appeared on the Idaho scene in 1893, exercising little influence on legislative deliberations in that year but successfully establishing their political distinctiveness.[53]

The 1895 and 1897 Idaho legislatures, especially the latter, were most fully indicative of the dimensions of mining state Populism. Memorials to Congress demanding the reestablishment of silver coinage, numerous bills to regulate wage payments, proposals to eliminate the "truck" system and to proscribe blacklisting of discharged employees, liberalization of bankruptcy and foreclosure procedures, tax relief, measures to restrict the importation of aliens to work in the state, and demands to create a Board of Immigration and Labor comprised the legislative staples of Idaho Populism.[54] Bluntly stated, Idaho Populism involved the visceral issues of working conditions, employment security, and basically negative relief measures to assist those with no immediate employment. Agricultural legislation was uncommon except for matters pertaining to irrigation, and, compared to the plains states, proposals for land and railroad reform were infrequent.[55]

Idaho Populism was laced with internal contradictions. In the 1895 and 1897 legislative sessions the party's representatives sponsored more reform bills than Republicans and Democrats combined, but they also exhibited a marked ability to vote in contravention of their own handiwork. The legislature memorialized Congress in 1895 demanding the reestablishment of silver coinage on the pre-1873 basis, for example, and all of the votes cast against the memorial were Populist votes.[56] Of thirty reform bills introduced in the legislatures of 1895 and 1897, twenty-three were Populist sponsored, six were approved, including three of Populist sponsorship, and most of the successful legislation concerned matters of marginal ideological consequence —restrictions on alien settlement in the state, regulation of irrigation water, wage payments in legal tender, and a reformed mechanic's lien law.[57] Populists never quite controlled the legislature, although in 1897 the coalition (combining both houses) of twenty-three Populists and eighteen Democrats easily outstripped the twenty-eight Silver Republicans. But the coalition shattered under the stress of legislative pressures, and in Idaho, as elsewhere, the insurgent threat to the established order was illusory.

Idaho's Populists achieved unity only in their demand for fiscal retrenchment and their intransigence concerning even the most minuscule budgetary items. Indeed, they pressed for sizeable reductions in every aspect of state appropriations, from the governor's stationery fund to postage allowances for state officers to the mileage rates allowed sheriffs in the return of escaped prisoners to funds for penitentiary and asylum improvements. Regarding a proposed $10,000 expenditure for prison and mental hospital improvements, for example, the Populists objected to the appropriation on the amazing grounds that inmates already possessed greater security than the unincarcerated poor. Diminished expenditures, in the estimation of the Idaho Populusts, would permit tax reductions and benefit the working citizens. They managed to avoid the question of how tax cuts might benefit the considerable body of unemployed miners deprived of an income with which to pay any taxes. Hence Idaho's People's party was a vehicle for the interests of employed, not unemployed, workingmen.[58]

Montana, another state in which Populism served principally to represent mine laborers, was influenced considerably less than Idaho. Populism took party form in 1892, but the established parties retained control of the Montana legislature despite the Populist challenge, reform proposals were few in number and marginal in impact, and the state's only Populist (fusionist) governor, Robert Burns Smith, rejoined the Democratic ranks after one term in office. Working conditions in the mines, wages and hours reform, economy in the administration of the state, and especially the free coinage of silver represented the primary demands of Montana Populists. Hence the questions of the regulation of hours of labor, the form of wage payments, conditions in the mines and smelting plants, and the safety and inspection of mines eclipsed such issues as railroad reform and anti-trust agitation. Few of the Populist demands were met in the 1897 session, and with the exception of an eight-hour day for hoisting engineers, an enactment requiring additional safety devices in mine shafts and a union label law for official state printing, Montana's Populist experience served primarily to add further impetus to the cause of free silver.[59]

On the other hand, Populism in Washington showed a clear affinity with the movement in Colorado, owing to a mixed constituency of farmers and labor members in the party in both of these states. The People's Party in Washington, in part the outgrowth of a durable Farmer's Alliance in the state, was organized at Ellensburg in 1892, but its electoral success in that year was negligible. In 1894 the party captured twenty seats in the state Legislature and secured control of a number of County Boards. Reduction of the "high" salaries of public officials represented one of the most consistent and enduring of Populist demands in Washington, but the party succeeded in its appeal only in 1896 and only as a result of wholesale fusion with the Democrats.[60]

However slightly, the Populist experience in Washington reflected a labor orientation. Legal protection for union members, anti-blacklisting bills, proposals to prohibit the "truck system" of wage payment, and mechanic's lien bills were basic to the reform effort in the state. In the fusionist legislature of 1897, Populists secured the enactment of a bill to create a Bureau of Labor and a mine and factory inspection measure. But Republicans contributed two mechanic's lien laws and an anti-wage garnishment act to the labor cause in the same session.[61] Other reforms, such as the prohibition of railroad passes and the establishment of fixed passenger fares were spurned by the Populists themselves.[62]

The reform potential of the Populists who controlled the 1897 legislature in Washington was negated by the bitter intra-party conflict over railroad regulation, a conflict nearly identical to that which ensued in the Kansas legislature in the same year. The advocacy of legally established maximum rates for freight traffic by the intransigent mid-road (anti-fusion) Populists and the moderate, fusionist group's desire for a railroad commission equipped with flexible rate-making authority proved to be irreconcilable positions.[63] This fundamental cleavage, coupled with the inexperience of the Populist legislators, only a few of whom had previous law-making experience, resulted in party war which stymied the legislature.[64] Moreover, Populist control of the legislature was not guaranteed, for the party held 45 of 78 House seats but only 15 of 34 Senate seats, the remainder divided between the sometimes hostile Democrats and Silver Republicans.[65] Eventually an unpopular and unworkable maximum rate bill cleared the legislature and secured the governor's signature, but pro-railroad forces amended the rate structure to the point that the maximum rates were not regarded as unprofitable. John R. Rogers, the Populist governor, affixed his signature to the bill because it was the only railroad bill the legislature could produce.[66]

Rogers' personal reform program was likewise emasculated. Tax reform, the governor's proposal to reduce the salaries of state officers, a measure to print and distribute school textbooks, and his unique plan to guarantee a $2,500 tax exempt homestead to all families failed to elicit support.[67] But the governor's promise to deliver an "honest, conservative administration" was a promise adhered to with tenacity, and if fiscal restraint is the true measure of conservatism, then Rogers surely succeeded. The state budget was trimmed by $1,000,000 — or nearly 50% — as compared to the previous biennium, and state services were obviously thoroughly reduced. In moves similar to the Nebraska experience, Washington Populists secured major appropriations reductions for the penal and geriatric institutions, and only the state soldiers home emerged financially unscathed.[68] And yet, however unsuccessfully, Populists did initiate about sixty per cent of the reform legislation in the 1897 session.[69]

If Populists shared a predominant attribute in all of the western states it was the common propensity for governmental frugality and budgetary retrenchment. The retrenchment priorities, of course, took variant forms in different states. In Idaho Populists pressed for across-the-board reduction in all areas of state expenditure, while in Montana the Populist governor, Robert Burns Smith, merely warned the Republican legislature of 1897 that he would not tolerate deficit financing for any reason.[70] Populists in Washington and Nebraska achieved cost reductions for penal, corrective and geriatric institutions, and in Washington the Populist governor, John R. Rogers, was especially interested in decreasing the state's expenditure on higher education. Though Rogers himself had authored the state's "barefoot schoolboy law" of 1895, a measure which equalized spending for rural and urban school districts, he developed special grievances with the normal schools which trained the teachers. Rogers observed that "teachers, like poets, are born and not made. Let us have as few colleges for the less than one-tenth of our youth who attend them as possible."[71] And in Colorado the Waite administration secured legislative approval for a fifteen per cent reduction in general state outlays.[72]

Debt, deficits and the costs of bureaucracy evoked flat condemnation in Populist circles, and the few ostensible exceptions to this norm, such as the advocacy of railroad regulatory commissions, were in reality not inconsistent with this posture. Populists believed that institutions and enterprises which were uncontrollable within the context of a natural competitive order should be extricated from the market altogether. And the most intransigent Populists pressed for the least expensive kind of regulatory solution — by statute or legal fiat. Government ownership of such non-competitive enterprises as the railroads commanded far less support among Populists than generally supposed. Only in one state, and on one occasion, was a memorial favoring government

ownership and operation of the railroad system ever approved by Populist legislators.[73] On this issue, as on so many others, Populists exhibited a fundamental ambivalence.

Nevertheless, Populism reflected some important structural characteristics
which have been little recognized. The party, for example, was more consistently reformist in the mountain states than elsewhere, and it operated in
these states almost exclusively as a vehicle of the aspirations of wage laborers
in the mining industry. Moreover, the party was neither as reformist as its
partisans contended, nor were the Republican legislators in Populist-influenced states as impervious to reform as Populists seemed to believe. Even on
the issue of railroad regulation, an issue upon which Populist behavior was the
most consistent, Populist originality must be regarded as dubious, for considerable sentiment in favor of the elimination of abuses existed within the railroad industry itself.[74]

The most that can be said for Populist state legislators is that as representatives of a new and short-lived political coalition their problems of identi-
ty, the definition of legitimate self-interest, and inner harmony were as understandable as their failures to resolve them. Populism was a disparate and
oftentimes incompatible alliance of the disenchanted, and the People's Party
utterly failed to engender the disciplinary mechanisms necessary to insure a
modicum of unity in legislative situations. In many legislative instances the
Populists held the balance of power and found themselves so disunited that
their power was negligible.

A substantially comprehensive compendium of reform legislation considered in the legislatures of Populist-influenced states during the period 1891-
1897 is presented in the following Table. A summary and an analysis of this
legislation, with the analysis in the form of an appendix, follow the Table.

TABLE I
TABLE OF REFORM MEASURES IN SEVEN POPULIST–INFLUENCED STATES
1891-1897[1]

Legislative Body	Terms of Bill	Sponsorship	Disposition[a]
1. Railroad Bills with Multifaceted Provisions			
Nebraska House, 1891 (966)[b]	Freight classification and maximum Rates	Independent[c]	3
Nebraska Senate, 1891 (358)	Reform of weighing and receipt provisions	Democratic	1
Nebraska House, 1893 (313)	Remedies for persons injured by railroad's negligence	Independent	4
Nebraska Senate, 1893 (161)	Extension of regulations to express companies	Republican	1
Nebraska Senate, 1895 (246)	Maximum rates for Pullman cars	Republican	1
Nebraska Senate, 1897 (582)	Regulation of Express Carrying	Democratic	3
Colorado Senate, 1893 (402)	Rate Regulation, Create Commission, Forbid Discrimination, Publication of Rate Schedules	Populist	1
Colorado House, 1893 (319)	Same Provisions as Senate Bill	Populist	1
Idaho House, 1893 (97)	Rate Regulation and Creation of Commission	Populist	1
South Dakota Senate, 1897 (274)	Regulation and Commission	Populist	4
Kansas House, 1891 (2 bills) (713, 624)	Establish Commission and Establish Maximum Rates for Freight and passenger Carriage	Republican / Alliance	2 / 2
Kansas Senate, 1893 (513)	Maximum Freight and Passenger Rates, Establish Commission; Forbid Discrimination	Populist	2
Idaho House, 1897 (21)	Regulation and Commission	Populist	1*
2. Railroad Bills: Maximum Passenger Rates			
Kansas Senate, 1897 (45)	Maximum Fares	Populist	1*
Nebraska Senate, 1897 (179)	Maximum Fares	Independent	1*
Washington Senate, 1897 (70)	Maximum Fares	Populist	1*

Idaho House, 1893 (28)	Maximum Fares	Populist	1
Idaho House, 1897 (95)	Maximum Fares	Populist	1*
Idaho Senate, 1897 (119)	Maximum Fares	Populist	1*
South Dakota House, 1897 (58)	Maximum Fares	Populist	1*
Washington House, 1897 (122)	Maximum Fares	Populist	1*

3. *Railroad Bills: Establishment of Maximum Freight Rates*

Nebraska House, 1891 (455)	Maximum Rates	Republican	1
Nebraska House, 1893 (706)	Rate Maximums and freight classification	Independent	4
Nebraska House, 1893 (675)	Establishment of maximum rates	Republican	1
Nebraska Senate, 1893 (346)	Maximum rates for transportation of livestock, grain, & other materials	Republican	1
Nebraska Senate, 1893 (574)	Reasonable maximum rates	Independent	1
Washington House, 1897 (992)	Establishment of Maximum Rates	Populist	4
Washington Senate, 1897 (635)	Establishment of Maximum Rates	Populist	1*
South Dakota House, 1897 (678)	Maximum Freight Rates	Populist	1*
Montana House, 1897 (102)	Maximum Freight Rates	Populist	1*
Kansas Senate, 1897 (640)	Maximum Freight Rates	Populist	4

4. *Railroad Bills: Establishment of or Extension of Powers of, Railroad Regulatory Commissions*

| Colorado House, 1893. (176) | Establishment of regulatory Commission | Republican | 1 |
| Washington House, 1897 (376) | Establishment of Railroad Commission | Populist | 1* |

5. *Railroad Bills: Prohibition of Free Passes*

Nebraska House, 1891 (739)	Prohibition of Free Passes for Passenger Travel	Independent	1*
Nebraska House, 1893 (890)	Prohibition of Free Passes for Passenger Travel	Independent	1
Nebraska House, 1895 (223)	Prohibition of Free Passes for	Independent	1

Nebraska House, 1897 (2 bills) (173) (288)	Prohibition of Free Passes for Passenger Travel	Independent Republican	1* 1
Nebraska Senate, 1897 (120)	Prohibition of Free Passes for Passenger Travel	Independent	1*
Montana House, 1897 (64)	Prohibition of Free Passes for Passenger Travel	Populist	1*
Washington Senate, 1897 (69)	Prohibition of Free Passes for Passenger Travel	Populist	1*
Idaho House, 1897 (92)	Prohibition of Free Passes for Passenger Travel	Populist	1*
Kansas House, 1891 (125)	Prohibition of Free Passes for Passenger Travel	Alliance	1*
South Dakota House, 1897 (235)	Prohibition of Free Passes for Passenger Travel	Populist	1*

6. Monetary and Legal Tender Bills and Petitions

Nebraska Senate, 1893 (95)	Bill to Create Legal Tender Currency in Nebraska	Independent	1
Nebraska House, 1897 (715)	Bill defining Legal Tender	Republican	2
Colorado House, 1893 (32)	Resolution on Free Coinage of Silver	Republican	–adopted
Colorado Senate, 1893 (138)	Bill defining gold *and* silver as Legal Tender	Populist	4
Colorado House, 1894 (148)	Bill to prohibit discrimination against different kinds of money	Populist	1
Idaho Senate, 1895 (26)	Memorial favoring free coinage of silver	Committee	4

7. Reform of Fiscal and Electoral Procedures

Nebraska House, 1893 (164)	Sponsorship of Inheritance Tax	Republican	1
Nebraska House, 1897 (721)	Prevent use of corporate money to influence elections	Independent	4
Nebraska House, 1897 (559)	Inheritance Tax	Independent	1*
Nebraska House, 1897 (992)	Guarantee of secret ballot	Republican	3
Nebraska Senate, 1897 (2 bills) (158 (250)	Prohibition of corrupt electoral practices	Democratic Republican	1 1
Washington Senate, 1897 (465)	Memorial on Direct Election of Senators	Democratic	–adopted
South Dakota House, 1897 (1275)	Secret Ballot	Populist	4
Colorado House, 1893 (181)	Memorial on Income Tax	Populist	–adopted

8. *Agricultural Legislation: Tax Relief; Reform of Foreclosure and Redemption Proceedings; Establishment of Maximum Rates of Interest*

Nebraska House, 1891 (188)	Suspension of laws relative to collection of delinquent taxes	Republican	1
Nebraska House, 1891 (293)	Amendment of foreclosure laws	Independent	1*
Nebraska House, 1891 (149)	Refulation of Rates of Interest	Independent	1*
Nebraska Senate, 1891 (142)	Redemption of property sold at judicial sale	Independent	1*
Nebraska House, 1897 (897)	Amend foreclosure and redemption proceedings to liberalize rights of persons involved in same	Democratic	2
Nebraska House, 1897 (494)	Relief of farmers from unequal tax burden on income	Democratic	1
Idaho House, 1895 (80)	Memorial favoring federal bankruptcy law	Joint Committee	4
Idaho Senate, 1895 (60)	Prohibit deficiency judgments in foreclosure cases	Populist	1
Idaho Senate, 1897 (35)	Relief for delinquent taxpayers	Populist	2*
Colorado House, 1894 (210)	Regulation of Interest Rates	Populist	1
Kansas House, 1891 (522)	Definition of Usury and Establishment of Maximum Interest Rates	Alliance	2
Kansas House, 1891 (16)	Redemption of Property sold at judicial sale	Republican	1
Kansas House, 1897 (48)	Regulation of Interest Rates	Populist	1*

9. *Regulatory Legislation: Commodities trading; Stockyards; Anti-Trust Bills; Police*

Nebraska House, 1891 (496)	Prohibition of gambling in stocks, bonds and commodities	Republican	2
Nebraska House, 1891 (508)	Regulation of stockyards	Independent	1*
Nebraska House, 1891 (962)	Prohibition of Combinations, pools and trusts	Republican	1
Nebraska Senate, 1891 (1031)	Creation and regulation of public warehouses and (agricultural) storage facilities	Democratic	3
Nebraska House, 1893 (323)	Regulation of Pinkertons and special police	Independent	2
Nebraska House, 1893 (594)	Stockyards Regulation	Republican	4
Nebraska House, 1893 (650)	Prohibition of price-fixing in lumber and coal	Republican	4
Nebraska House, 1893 (560)	Warehouse and grain grading regulation	Independent	1

Nebraska Senate, 1893 (501)	Refulation of importation of armed special police	Independent	3
Nebraska Senate, 1893 (419)	Prohibition of gambling in commodities futures	Independent	1
Nebraska House, 1895 (2 bills) (143) (905)	Regulation and Inspection of Stockyards	Democratic Republican	1 2
Nebraska House, 1895 (1132)	Creation of State Banking Board	Republican	4
Nebraska Senate, 1895 (868)	Prohibition of Bucket Shops and gambling in securities	Republican	2
Nebraska House, 1897 (1040)	Prohibition of combinations in grain elevator business	Republican	4
Nebraska House, 1897 (493)	Anti-trust bill	Independent	1*
Nebraska Senate, 1897 (452)	Stockyards regulation	Independent	4
Nebraska Senate, 1897 (571)	Prohibition of trusts and conspiracies to restrain trade	Democratic	3
Washington House, 1897 (188)	Anti-trust and conspiracies in restraint of trade	Republican	1
Idaho House, 1893 (160)	Regulation of mining corporations	Populist	2
Kansas House, 1891 (75)	Stockyards regulation	Alliance	1*
Kansas House, 1891 (266)	Regulation of weighing of coal at mine, i.e., coal screening	Alliance	3
Kansas Senate, 1891 (476)	Prohibition of combinations in livestock commission business	Republican	4
Kansas Senate, 1897 (789)	Stockyards and livestock commission regulation	Populist	1*
South Dakota Senate, 1897 (525)	Prevention of Monopolies and trusts	Populist	4
Kansas Senate, 1897 (186)	Anti-trust bill	Populist	1*
Kansas House, 1897 (197)	Anti-trust bill	Populist	1*
Kansas Senate, 1891 (480)	Warehouse inspection; Inspection of weighing and handling grain	Republican	4
Kansas House, 1897 (90)	Amend warehouse and grain inspection law	Populist	1*

10. *Labor Legislation: Wages, Hours, Conditions of Employment*   .

Nebraska House, 1891 (1268)	Prohibition of "yellow-dog" contracts	Democratic	4
Nebraska House, 1891 (296)	Employers' Liability and Compensation for Injury	Republican	1
Nebraska House, 1891 (307)	Eight-hour day on state projects	Democratic	1
Nebraska House, 1893 (853)	Anti-sweatshop bill	Democratic	4
Nebraska House, 1893 (389)	Guarantee of right to union membership	Independent	1
Nebraska House, 1893 (671)	Weekly compensation bill	Independent	1
Nebraska House, 1893 (561)	Establishment of public employment offices	Democratic	1
Nebraska House, 1895 (130)	Establishment of public employment offices	Republican	1
Nebraska House, 1895 (190)	Anti-sweatshop bill	Independent	1
Nebraska Senate, 1895 (198)	Prohibition of blacklisting	Republican	1
Nebraska House, 1897 (355)	Disallowance of negligence by fellow employee as rationale by employers in job injury lawsuits	Democratic	1
Nebraska Senate, 1897 (183)	Anti-blacklisting bill	Republican	1
Colorado House, 1894 (271)	Regulation of hours of labor of mechanics	Populist	1
Colorado House, 1893 (173)	Regulation of Wage Payments	Democratic	1
Colorado House, 1893 (175)	Regulation of hours of labor	Populist	1
Washington House, 1897 (364)	Protection of miners underground; mine and factory inspection	Populist	4
Washington House, 1897 (19)	Anti-wage garnishment bill	Republican	4
Washington House, 1897 (404)	Creation of Bureau of Labor	Populist	4
Washington Senate, 1897 (103)	Anti-blacklisting bill	Populist	1*
Idaho House, 1895 (70)	Regulation of hours of labor	Republican	1
Idaho House, 1895 (82)	Prohibition of truck system	Populist	1
Idaho House, 1895 (162)	Regulation of hours of labor in mines	Populist	2
Idaho House, 1895 (186)	Regulation of wage payments	Populist	4

Idaho Senate, 1895 (110)	Regulation of wage payments	Populist	1
Idaho Senate, 1895 (110)	Anti-blacklisting bill	Populist	1
Idaho Senate, 1897 (13)	Regulation of hours in mines and smelting plants	Democratic	1
Idaho Senate, 1897 (82)	Payment of wages in lawful money, i.e., prohibition of truck system	Populist	1*
Idaho Senate, 1897 (47)	Anti-blacklisting bill	Populist	1*
Kansas House, 1891 (26)	Weekly pay bill	Alliance	1*
Kansas House, 1891 (62)	Eight-hour day on state and municipal projects	Alliance	1*
Kansas Senate, 1891 (732)	Eight-hour day on state and municipal projects	Republican	4
Kansas Senate, 1891 (83)	Prohibition of child labor under age of 14	Republican	1
Kansas Senate, 1893 (555)	Weekly pay in lawful money	Populist	4
Kansas Senate, 1893 (39)	Anti-garnishment bill	Populist	1*
Kansas Senate, 1893 (304)	Prohibition of child labor under age of 14	Populist	1*
Kansas House, 1893 (55)	Anti-wage garnishment bill	Republican	1
Kansas House, 1897 (46)	Weekly wages in lawful money	Democratic	1
Kansas House, 1897 (46)	Prevention of discrimination against members of labor unions	Democratic	1
Kansas House, 1897 (55)	Anti-blacklisting bill	Republican	1
Kansas Senate, 1897 (71)	Anti-blacklisting bill	Populist	1*

11. *Labor Legislation: Lien Bills*

Nebraska House, 1891 (962)	Mechanic's Lien Bill	Republican	1
Colorado Senate, 1893 (242)	Mechanic's Lien Bill	Republican	4
Washington Senate, 1897 (244)	Mechanic's Lien Bill	Republican	4
Idaho House, 1893 (57)	Mechanic's Lien Bill	Republican	4
South Dakota House, 1897 (325)	Farm laborer's lien bill	Populist	1*
Idaho House, 1897 (21)	Reformed lien law	Democratic	4

12. *Land Legislation*

Nebraska House, 1891 (356)	Bill to restrict land ownership of non-resident aliens	Independent	1*
Nebraska House, 1891 (509)	Bill to prevent foreign persons or corporations from acquiring land for speculative purposes	Independent	1*
Idaho House, 1893 (139)	Bill to forbid foreign ownership of Idaho real estate	Republican	1
Kansas House, 1891 (18)	Bill to restrict foreign ownership of real estate	Republican	1
Kansas Senate, 1891 (200)	Bill to restrict land ownership to citizens and aliens with declared citizenship intentions	Republican	4
Idaho Senate, 1897 (14)	Discouragement of further settlement of aliens in Idaho	Populist	4
Idaho House, 1897 (98)	Regulation of Irrigation water and rates charged therefore	Bipartisan	4

SUMMARY OF TABLE I

Type of Bill	Number	Sponsorship		Disposition of Populist Bills in House of Origin		Disposition of Populist Bills in Populist or Fusionist Controlled houses	
		Populist	Non-Populist	Passed	Failed	Passed	Failed
Railroad (Sections 1-5)	45	35	10	8	27	6	20
Monetary, Fiscal, Electoral (Sections 6-7)	15	7	8	4	3	2	1
Agricultural, Regulatory (Sections 8-9)	42	23	19	8	15	4	12
Labor (Sections 10-11)	46	22	24	5	17	3	9
Land Reform (Section 12)	7	3	4	1	2	1	2
TOTAL	155	90 (58%)	65 (42%)	26 (29%)	64 (71%)	16 (27%)	44 (73%)

Sources and Notes to Table I:

Sources: *House and Senate Journals* for the following states and legislative sessions: Nebraska, 1891, 1893, 1895, 1897; Kansas, 1891, 1893, 1895, 1897; Idaho, 1893, 1895, 1897; Colorado, 1893, 1894; Washington, 1897; Montana, 1897; South Dakota, 1897.

Notes: a *Key to Table I:* 1=bill not considered, buried in committee or defeated in House of origin; 2=passed House of origin, not acted upon, buried in committee or defeated in other House; 3=passed both Houses and successfully vetoed or not acted upon by governor; 4=enacted into law. Asterisk* indicates a Populist sponsored bill which failed in a Populist or fusionist controlled House. (Duplicate bills sponsored by members of the same party and bills withdrawn from consideration in deference to similar bills are not included in the table.)

b Full documentation of the legislative materials in this table would yield a plethora of digits not unlike a table of random numbers. The reader is therefore referred to the numbers in parentheses which appear with the designated legislative body in the stub of the table. These digits represent the page number in the appropriate legislative journal in which a bill was either introduced or voted upon. This pagination will refer the reader to the crucial aspect in the life of a bill. In the majority of cases the reference is to the introduction.

c Nebraska Populists were designated as Independents (later People's Independents) in the legislature. Kansas bills with "Alliance" sponsorship are considered to be Populist bills.

APPENDIX TO TABLE I

The legislative material noted in Table I and its Summary reveals important facts about the reform context in which the Populists functioned. The Table demonstrates that reformism in the plains region was basically agrarian, but it also indicates a labor stratum of significant import. It reveals that mountain state reform was principally laborite rather than silver-oriented. And, most importantly, it shows that, if railroad measures are excluded from consideration, Populists were no more likely to be sponsors of reform measures than non-Populists. Moreover, it indicates that Populist-sponsored measures fared poorly in the legislative process and that Populist bills were no more likely to pass Populist controlled legislative bodies than assemblies in which Populists were in the minority.

Roll call analysis might be expected to yield further insights into the disposition of reform bills. Unfortunately this is rarely the case. Populist bills bearing a designation of "1," i.e., failed in the House of origin, in Table I failed in all but one instance to reach the voting stage. A "skill in legislative management" index, if such a tool existed, would undoubtedly reveal more than roll-call analysis. Yet, if Table I demonstrates that, with the exception of railroad reform, Populists were no more likely to be sponsors of reform than non-Populists, it should not be surprising that reform measures which were brought to a vote were normally enacted with little or no evidence of partisan cleavage. This was the case in all but a few discrete instances, generally those in which debtor and creditor interests were placed in explicit confrontation— railroad bills, mortgage foreclosure and interest rate bills, and memorials and petitions on coinage or fiscal policy. Even with respect to these issues partisanship had dissipated considerably by 1896.

For example, note the voting patterns on the following proposals. Indicating the vote only in the sponsoring House (the other chamber voting similarly, if at all), the Kansas Senate of 1891 voted the eight hour day on state projects by 26-2, the 1893 Kansas Senate approved a weekly pay bill by 27-0, and in 1897 the Kansas Senate favored maximum railroad rates by 40-0. The Idaho House in 1893 approved a bill to regulate mining corporations by 29-4, the Senate of that State in 1895 memorialized Congress in favor of free silver by 15-3 (all negative votes were cast by Populists!), and in 1897 the Idaho Senate voted to restrict further settlement of "aliens" in the state by 26-7, with the negatives split among three parties. In 1897 the South Dakota Senate favored railroad regulation by 40-0 and approved anti-trust legislation 41-1. The Washington Senate of the same year legislated maximum railroad freight rates by 31-2, and the 1897 Nebraska House forbade the corrupt use of corporate money to influence elections by an 84-1 vote. When reform legislation did come to vote, that legislation, whether Populist or non-Populist in sponsorship, was normally enacted by overwhelming non-partisan majorities such as those in the examples cited above.

Sharp partisan cleavages, however, did manifest themselves in the Colorado legislative sessions of 1893 and 1894 and on railroad, mortgage foreclosure and interest rate bills in Kansas and Nebraska, especially in the early years of Populist legislative presence. These cleavages may be demonstrated by employing the (Rice) *Index of Party Likeness* to indicate partisanship and the (Rice) *Index of Party Cohesion* to measure party solidarity on significant roll calls. Roll calls on the following bills represent the most demonstrable instances of party disagreement in the plains and mountain states during the Populist period, 1891-1897.

APPENDIX TO TABLE I

Likeness and Cohesion Indices re: Selected Roll Calls, 1891-1897

		Index of Likeness[a]		Index of Cohesion[b]		
Legislative Body	Terms of Bill	Pop.&Rep.	Pop.&Dem.	Rep.	Dem.	Pop.
Kansas House, 1891 (522)	Definition of Usury and establishment of maximum interest rates.	16	c	72	–	96
Kansas House, 1891 (624)	Establish Railroad Commission; establish maximum rates.	16	–	100	–	100
*Kansas House, 1891 (713)	Establish Railroad Commission; establish maximum rates.	5	–	91	–	100
Nebraska House,1891 (966)	Railroad Freight Classification and Maximum rates.	76	48	53	4	100
Nebraska House,1891 (1181)	Memorial Favoring Government ownership of railroads.	33	33	33	38	98
Nebraska House,1893 (706)	Railroad Rate maximums and freight classification.	39	73	22	46	100
Nebraska House,1893 (313)	Remedies for persons injured by railroad's negligence	59	100	18	100	100
*Nebraska House,1897 (715)	Bill defining legal tender.	22	91	56	81	100
Nebraska House,1897 (897)	Amend foreclosure and redemption proceedings to liberalize rights of persons involved in same.	33	84	39	63	96
Colorado House, 1893 (265)	Memorial favoring federal income tax.	24	100	52	100	100
Colorado House, 1894 (271)	Regulation of hours of labor of mechanics & others	44	67	65	20	46

Sources: Legislative journals for the pertinent legislative assembly and biennial sessions. Page references appear in parentheses in the stub of the table. Asterisks indicate a non-Populist bill.

Notes to Appendix Table I:

a The *index of likeness* is determined by calculating the percentage of members of each party voting in favor of a bill, subtracting the smaller percentage from the larger, and subtracting that remainder from 100. Index values range from 0 to 100, and the smaller the index value the greater the party split on a roll call. (Numerical scores have been rounded to the nearest whole number.)

b The *index of cohesion* is computed by ascertaining the percentage of yeas and nays cast by members of the same party on a roll call and subtracting the smaller percentage from the larger. Index values range from 0 to 100, with high values indicating party solidarity and low values revealing intra-party disagreement. (Numerical scores have been rounded to the nearest whole number.)

c Blank spaces in the Table indicate insignificant voting representation by members of a party on a roll call.

It is clear that on a few basic issues Populists exhibited nearly complete voting cohesion. This unanimity or near unanimity was remarkably in contrast to their normal inability to bring bills to a vote, even in legislative bodies in which they were dominant. Hence it may have been true that the Populist problem was inept legislative management rather than intra-party conflict, but, given the absence of recorded legislative debates and committee hearings which might illuminate the matter, the point must remain moot. And the original conclusion remains unaffected—except on railroad regulation issues Populists were no more reformist than Republicans (or Democrats), and the demonstrated reform concerns of Populists reflected a somewhat narrower emphasis than the reform interests of other parties. Nor did Populists expand their reform horizons during the brief history of the movement. If anything, their concerns narrowed.

CHAPTER SEVEN

The Futilitarians:
Western Populists in the House of Representatives, 1891-1900

The attitudes and performance of Populist congressmen from the western states provided further demonstration of the fundamentally conservative nature of Populism. Reform politicians, representing state-based People's Parties, or the Farmers Alliances, or officially styled as Independents, were first elected to the federal House in 1890, and members fitting the general designation of "Populist" served in the Fifty-second, Fifty-third, Fifty-fourth and Fifty-fifth Congresses. In numerical terms they were, of course, inconsequential, comprising eight, nine, seven, and twenty-six members in the four respective congresses, although a number of the latter group were "fusionists" whose Populist credentials were somewhat dubious.[1] Hence the congressional delegation of the People's Party consisted ordinarily of two per cent, and never more than seven per cent, of the full House Membership. And, since Democrats controlled the first two congresses by a considerable margin and Republicans dominated the last two by even larger margins, Populists were never able to play a brokerage or swing-group role in the House.

Moreover, the attenuated political careers of most of the Populist congressmen precluded the construction of an effective party strategy during the life of the movement. Only three Populists, William Baker and Jerry Simpson of Kansas and Omer Kem of Nebraska served in as many as three congresses; only two, Baker and Kem, served in three congresses consecutively, and only Simpson endured politically long enough to be present in both the Fifty-second and the Fifty-fifth Congresses.[2] The original delegation, elected in 1890, consisted of five Kansans, Baker, Simpson, John Davis, John Grant Otis and Benjamin H. Clover, two Nebraska Independents, Kem and William McKeighan, and Kittel Halvorson of Minnesota. Baker, Davis, Simpson, Kem and McKeighan won reelection in 1892, and William Alexander Harris replaced Clover in the Kansas contingent. But only Baker and Kem survived the Populist debacle of 1894 to carry the party's standard into the Fifty-fourth Congress as representatives from western states.[3]

Populist representation broadened in 1892 with the election of two Colorado congressmen, Lafayette Pence and John C. Bell. Bell repeated in 1894 as a Populist and served in three subsequent congresses as a Democrat. The voters obliterated most of the original western Populists in 1894, but four new representatives from the South, Harry Skinner and William Stroud of North Carolina and Milford Howard and Albert Goodwyn of Alabama, appeared in Congress to bolster the depleted ranks of their western colleagues.[4]

The election of 1894 and the subsequent period of the Fifty-fourth Congress comprised both the nadir of Populist influence and also marked a fundamental point of departure in the party experience. With the resurgence of Populist strength in 1896, occasioned by Populist-Democratic fusion at both state and federal levels, there emerged into positions of prominence in the party new men of markedly different background and experience. The differences, in fact, were sufficiently striking that it is plausible to offer the generalization that, in the national political realm, there were two Populist movements represented in the 1890s, one encompassing the years from 1890 to 1894, the other a transitory and chimera-like phenomenon which acquired prominence in 1896 and quickly faded from view, leaving few traces on the fabric of national politics.

This generalization may be supported by an examination of the composition and distribution of the Populists elected for the first (and last) time in 1896. In the congressional elections synonymous with the Bryan-McKinley campaign some twenty-six men with claims upon Populist endorsement won seats in the Fifty-fifth Congress. Sixteen of these congressmen-elect represented western states and ten others came from other regions, seven from the South, two from the Middle West, and one from Kentucky, a border state. For twenty-two of them, including fifteen of the sixteen westerners, the election of 1896 was the only time their *Populist* connections afforded them electoral success in federal politics. Only eleven of the twenty-six succeeded without the endorsement of the Democrats, and only four of these eleven represented western districts—two South Dakotans, one Kansan and one Nebraskan. The remaining twelve western Populists won election as fusion candidates.[5]

The Populist congressmen who faced the McKinley administration and its Republican majority in Congress bore little resemblance to the original Populists of 1890 who had originally carried the banner of reform to Washington. For example, the original eight Populists elected in 1890 consisted of eight practicing farmers. The Populists elected in 1892 consisted of seven farmers and two lawyers, while the 1894 group of seven, including four southerners, contained three farmers and four lawyers. In the Populist resurgence of 1896, largely attendant upon fusion with the Democrats, farmers—and the cause of agrarian reform—virtually disappeared from the scene. The sixteen western Populists who served in the Fifty-fifth Congress consisted of two clergymen, two merchants, four newspaper publishers, six attorneys, one physician and Jerry Simpson, a rancher. Two of the publishers, one of the clergymen and one of the lawyers specified farming as a secondary or ancillary occupation, but *none* of the sixteen were full-time crop-cultivating agriculturalists at the time of their election. Addition of the ten non-western Populists to the roster delineates further the demise of agrarians in the leadership of the party. These ten were comprised of one clergyman, one physician, one chemist, five lawyers, and only two practicing farmers.[6] Hence the discontinuity of background and occupational interest which separated the early and later congressional representatives of Populism is fundamental and nearly absolute. In summary form the relevant data are presented below.

TABLE I

WESTERN POPULISTS IN CONGRESS, 1891-1899

1. 52nd Congress, 1891-1893 (elected November, 1890)

Congressmen	State and District	Home	Birth	Occupation	Endorsement
William Baker	Kansas, 6th	Lincoln	Pennsylvania, 1831	farmer	People's Party
John G. Otis	Kansas, 4th	Topeka	Vermont, 1838	farmer	People's Party
Benjamin H. Clover	Kansas, 3rd	Cambridge	Ohio, 1837	farmer	People's Party
John Davis	Kansas, 5th	Junction City	Illinois, 1826	farmer	People's Party
Jerry Simpson	Kansas, 7th	Medicine Lodge	British North America, 1842	rancher	People's Party & Democratic
William McKeighan	Nebraska, 2nd	Red Cloud	New Jersey, 1842	farmer	Farmer's Alliance & Democratic
Omer Madison Kem	Nebraska, 3rd	Broken Bow	Indiana, 1855	farmer	Farmer's Alliance
Kittel Halvorson	Minnesota, 7th	Stearns County	Norway, 1846	farmer	Farmer's Alliance

2. 53rd Congress, 1893-1895 (elected November, 1892)

William Baker	------	------	------	------	------
John Davis	------	------	------	------	------
Jerry Simpson	------	------	------	------	------
Omer Madison Kem	------	------	------	------	------
William McKeighan	------	------	------	------	Independent
new members					
William Alexander Harris	Kansas, at large	Linwood	Virginia, 1841	farmer	Populist and Democratic
John C. Bell	Colorado, 2nd	Montrose	Tennessee, 1851	attorney (also judge)	Populist and Democratic
Lafayette Pence	Colorado, 1st	Denver	Indiana, 1857	attorney	Populist and Democratic
Haldor Boen	Minnesota, 7th	Fergus Falls	Norway, 1851	farmer	Populist

Mason Peters	Kansas, 2nd	Kansas City	Missouri, 1844	attorney (also merchant)	Populist and Democratic
Edwin Ridgely	Kansas, 3rd	Pittsburg	Illinois, 1844	merchant	Populist and Democratic
Jerry Simpson	Kansas, 7th	Medicine Lodge	British North America, 1842	rancher	Populist and Democratic
William L. Stark	Nebraska, 4th	Aurora	Connecticut, 1853	attorney (also judge)	Populist and Democratic
Roderick D. Sutherland	Nebraska, 5th	Nelson	Iowa, 1862	attorney	Populist and Democratic
William D. Vincent	Kansas, 5th	Clay Center	Tennessee, 1852	merchant	Populist and Democratic

3. 54th Congress, 1895-1897 (elected November, 1894)[a]

William Baker	-----	-----	-----	-----	-----
Omer Madison Kem	-----	-----	-----	-----	-----
John C. Bell	-----	-----	-----	-----	-----

4. 55th Congress, 1897-1899 (elected November, 1896)[b]

Charles A. Barlow	California, 6th	San Luis Obispo	Ohio, 1858	publisher (also farmer)	Populist and Democratic
Jeremiah Botkin	Kansas, at large	Winfield	Illinois, 1849	clergyman	Populist and Democratic
James Callahan	Oklahoma Territory, delegate	Kingfisher	Missouri, 1852	clergyman	Populist and Democratic
Curtis H. Castle	California, 7th	Merced	Illinois, 1848	physician	Populist and Democratic
William L. Greene	Nebraska, 6th	Kearney	Indiana, 1849	attorney (also judge)	Populist
James Gunn	Idaho, at large	Boise	Ireland, 1843	editor	Populist and Democratic
John E. Kelley	South Dakota, at large	Flandreau	Wisconsin, 1853	publisher and editor	Populist
Freeman Knowles	South Dakota, at large	Deadwood	Maine, 1846	publisher (also attorney)	Populist
Nelson McCormick	Kansas, 6th	Phillipsburg	Pennsylvania, 1847	attorney	Populist
Samuel Maxwell	Nebraska, 3rd	Fremont	New York, 1826	attorney	Populist and Democratic

Sources:

Congressional Directory, 52 Cong., 1 Sess.; 53 Cong., 1 Sess.; 54 Cong., 1 Sess.; 55 Cong., 3 Sess.; (Washington, 1891, 1893, 1896, 1898).

Populists from non-western states

a Populists from non-western states in the Fifty-fourth Congress were Albert Goodwyn and Milford Howard of Alabama and Harry Skinner and William Stroud of North Carolina.

b Non-western Populists in the Fifty-fifth Congress were the following: Jehu Baker of Illinois; Albert Todd of Michigan; John S. Rhea of Kentucky; John E. Fowler, Charles H. Martin, Alonzo Shuford, Harry Skinner and William Stroud, all of North Carolina; Thomas Jefferson Strait of South Carolina; Milford Howard of Alabama.

It appears, therefore, that the leadership of the Populist movement, distinctly agrarian in the beginning, gravitated rather quickly toward mercantile and professional people in the villages and towns of the western states. In this process the year 1894 and the severe electoral reverses suffered by the party appear to have been factors of fundamental consequence, and the leadership vacuum which materialized after the electoral debacle of 1894 permitted the penetration of the party apparatus by a new and differently-oriented element. To put it succinctly, politically ambitious village Democrats from mercantile or professional backgrounds served as an intrusive element during the hiatus period and assumed control of the party. Without doubt the fusion of Populists and Democrats operated as the efficacious variable in the agrarians' forfeiture of the leadership role in their own creation.

Thus, the men elected to the House in 1896 bearing the appellation of "Populist" represented an aberration, a marginal appendage to a movement the distinctive and meaningful form of which had been dissolved in the fusion process of 1894 to 1896. An assessment of the means and circumstances of Populist electoral victories in 1896 demonstrates this point clearly. Only four of the sixteen westerners elected in 1896 won without Democratic endorsement, and one of these, Nelson McCormick of Kansas, succeeded William Baker in a district uniformly Populist since 1890. The other three, John E. Kelley and Freeman Knowles of South Dakota and William L. Greene of Nebraska won election in districts in which no Democratic candidate appeared to complicate the contests. Moreover, Kelley and Knowles were *at large* candidates whose state-wide majorities were less than one per cent in a state swept by fusionist candidates for state offices. Of the remaining twelve, all of them elected as fusionists, four carried their districts by small pluralities in contests featuring several candidates, and five others succeeded by majorities of less than one per cent. Hence only three of the fusionists secured clear majorities. In sum, only two Populists, Greene of Nebraska and McCormick of Kansas, managed to win their seats both in the absence of Democratic endorsement *and* by majorities in excess of one per cent.[7] Clearly the last Populists were but passing shadows on the political scene.

Nevertheless, both the early Populists and the marginal delegation of 1896 failed to conform to the popular and contemporary stereotype of "Populist." As the prominence of professional men among the party's congressional representatives surely attested, the "hayseed" image of Populists was unwarranted.[8] And, if educational attainment affords a reasonable guide to political sophistication, then it must be conceded that Populist congressmen were the equals of their Republican and Democratic contemporaries. Consider, for example, the original Populist delegation from Kansas. William Baker, a farmer, held a degree from Waynesburg College in Pennsylvania, John Davis, another farmer, had graduated from Illinois College in Jacksonville, and John Grant Otis, the educational aristocrat of the group, possessed a B.A. from Williams and a law degree from Harvard. Baker had never practiced, but Otis, derisively termed the "Topeka milkman" by his adversaries, had abandoned his law office for a dairy farm. The educational experiences of Jerry Simpson, Benjamin Clover, Omer Kem and William McKeighan were confined to the "common schools," but Kittel Halvorson, though not a university man, had taught school for some years before acquiring his farm.[9]

Among the new Populist members of the Fifty-third Congress only Haldor Boen of Minnesota was a product solely of the common schools. William Alexander Harris of Kansas, internationally known for his achievements in the breeding of shorthorn cattle, was the son of a former Virginia congressman, a graduate of Virginia Military Institute, a civil engineer, an ex-colonel in the army of the Confederacy, and a scion of an old family whose Virginia landholdings derived from a grant made by William and Mary. In 1897 Harris was sent to the Senate as the successor of William A. Peffer, Kansas' first Populist senator.[10] Moreover, the two Colorado Populists elected in 1892 could boast of more than ordinary accomplishments. Lafayette Pence, an attorney, had graduated from Hanover College in Indiana and came to the House from a previous position as prosecuting attorney of Arapahoe County (Denver). John C. Bell, who defected to the Democrats after two terms as a Populist congressman, had served as a village mayor, county attorney and district judge before his election.[11]

Nor were the Populists elected to Congress in 1890 or 1892 newcomers to politics. Among the Kansans, for example, John Davis had twice campaigned for Congress as a Greenbacker, Jerry Simpson and Benjamin Clover had run for the state legislature on the Union Labor ticket, Clover had served as president of the Kansas Farmer's Alliance, and John Grant Otis had been state lecturer for the Grange. The two Nebraskans, Omer Kem and William McKeighan, had been county officers and Alliance officials. Kittel Halvorson of Minnesota was a veteran state legislator and his successor, Haldor Boen, was a former county commissioner and register of deeds. Lafayette Pence and John C. Bell of Colorado were elected judicial officers at the time of their election to Congress.[12]

Previous public experience of a political or judicial nature was also characteristic of the Populists elected in 1896 from Kansas, Nebraska, South Dakota, Idaho, California and Oklahoma Territory to serve in the Fifty-fifth Congress. Among the members of this delegation were four Nebraskans, William Greene, a district judge, Samuel Maxwell, a former state supreme court justice,

Roderick D. Sutherland, a county judge, and William Stark, a county judge and Judge Advocate General of the Nebraska National Guard. A number of others elected in 1896 possessed experience in state legislative chambers or county offices. And these congressmen held earned degrees from such institutions as Northwestern University, the University of Michigan, William Jewell and the Kansas State Agricultural College.[13]

In no sense did these congressmen fit the "calamity howler" stereotype of Populists. The credentials of the ten other Populists from the Middle West and South were at least equal to those of their western colleagues. Among the non-western Populist representatives in the Fifty-fifth Congress, for example, were a former three term congressman and United States Minister to Venezuela as well as professional men who held degrees from Wake Forest, Washington and Lee, the University of Kentucky and the University of Virginia.[14]

Nevertheless the *western* Populists in all of the congresses from 1891 to 1899 comprised a distinctive bloc within the party. This distinctiveness derived from the substantial incidence of involvement in dissident political movements antecedent to Populism which characterized many of the western congressmen and none of the other Populists. Three western Populists had previously sought office as candidates of the Prohibition party, three others had run as Greenbackers, two more had campaigned as Union Labor party candidates, another functioned as an organizer for the militant Western Federation of Miners, and a number of others sought office in local elections as independents or Alliance candidates.[15] Long term disenchantment with the control and conduct of public affairs, and sustained ideological wanderlust, was apparently commonplace among the westerners. Populism served as one phase, ordinarily the last phase, in a prolonged political and philosophical quest.

This deep-seated dissatisfaction with "the system" also explains the commonplace role which western Populists played in Congress even without a consciously formulated strategy or the guidance of a disciplined caucus—the role of broad-gauged social critics rather than conscious servants of the agrarian and labor interests which elected them to office. Indeed, the western Populists devoted little, strikingly little, attention and energy to the specifics of agricultural or labor matters. As depression era politicians their efforts reflected concern for the formulation of policies conducive to the restoration of general conditions of prosperity rather than the advocacy of palliatives for particular labor or agricultural problems. Considering their powerless position in the Congress this was undoubtedly a prudent strategy, for Populist-sponsored legislative bills were invariably consigned to committees from which they never emerged. Yet even on a philosophical level their behavior was predestined, for the Populist congressmen were incapable of serving the causes of special interests, even the special interests who had sent them to Washington.

In spite of their numerous personal peculiarities the western Populists exhibited a remarkable unanimity of attitude, although the subsequent careers of many of them failed to reflect a continuity of conviction. Their world-view was quite uniform, and it was also broad enough to permit all kinds of evidence to be incorporated into a standardized and predictable pattern of analysis. They interpreted the real world as constitutive of a vast dualism, with clear lines of demarcation separating the powerful and the powerless, the producers and the non-producers, or, to employ one of their characteristic expressions, the robbers and the robbed.[16] Moreover, the Populist analysis of power in the world involved a belief in the existence of certain tightly constructed economic linkages leading from dominant institutions in the United States to even more potent powers in the United Kingdom which, in the end, controlled all economic relationships of consequence in the western world. Anglophobia was patent and explicit among the westerners. As Curtis H. Castle, a colorful and loquacious California Populist phrased it: "Rothschild controls Morgan, Morgan controls Hanna, and Hanna controls McKinley, the Supreme Court, the Senate and the House of Representatives. Hanna is America."[17]

This assessment of reality did not necessarily mean that Populists interpreted the political and economic processes in terms of an ongoing and surreptitious "conspiracy" of bankers, financiers, and corporate interests to squeeze the powerless producing classes. The robbers already owned the world. They had no reason to conspire to acquire power which they all too obviously possessed. Only periodic adjustments among the robbers, prompted by new opportunities and unforeseen crises, were necessary to maintain their vise-like grip on the producing classes. Populists used such terms as "plot" and "collusion" with some regularity, but these usages were normally employed in describing the activities of small and subordinate constituents of the gigantic robber machine such as elevator companies or individual railroads. Tranquillity reigned at the Rothschild-Morgan level, and Lombard and Wall Streets remained undisturbed. Only incredible and unpredictable contingencies, such as the massive gold drain from the United States in the Cleveland administration, necessitating the flotation of issues of "gold bonds" in Europe, or the rare opportunity afforded by manipulation of the finance plans during the Spanish-American War, were of sufficient consequence to rouse the robber elite from their torpor.[18]

Populist congressmen constructed a clear and discerning analysis of the manner in which existing institutions and public policies were contoured to exploit and humiliate the producing masses, an analysis which rested, of course, upon assumptions which an obvious majority of their contemporaries declined to accept. Such convictions as "Hanna is America" were more than rhetorical glosses contrived for political effect. But the rhetorical and analytical propensities of the western Populists did point directly to their primary deficiencies as congressmen—their collective predilection to devote most of their energies to analysis rather than to advocacy. Their concern was to identify problems and analyze contemporary reality rather than to serve as effective instruments of change.

With remarkable singleness of mind western Populists identified the preeminent problem in America as the existence of an all-embracing and multifaceted monopoly. In order to preserve their exclusivist position, moreover, the forces of monopoly skillfully manufactured and exploited sham issues to confuse and becloud the public's image of reality and to deflect attention from the central issue of monopoly. To Populists the singular cause of depressed economic conditions in the 1890s and the attendant hardships imposed upon their constituents by the depression could not be located in such prominent smokescreen issues as the tariff, nor in general fiscal policy, nor in the notion that overproduction afflicted the economy. The cause was money monopoly and the perpetuation of a monetary policy which guaranteed a chronic shortage of currency. In their emphasis upon the dominant role of monetary factors in the business cycle Populists anticipated the later "Keynesian" analysis by a generation. Technically, Populist advocacy of currency expansion as an anti-depression tool took several forms—the restoration of silver coinage, the issuance of treasury notes, a combination of both of these devices, and even, in the end, an expansion of gold coinage.[19] Moreover, the demand for currency expansion represented more than a manifestation of the typical agrarian debtor's propensity for inflationary panaceas predicated upon a naive conception of the quantity theory of money. To Populist congressmen currency expansion was the central concept of their intellectual world, the only feasible device to restore prosperous conditions, and the key to economic relationships and social tranquillity.

Hence Populists believed that the preeminent enemies of the working people were the great American and British banking houses, while industrial corporations and railroads, most of which were subordinate to the bankers in any event, constituted comparatively minor nuisances. In the banking community were to be found the efficacious agents of currency contraction and the partisans of the naturally deflationary gold standard. The totally self-interested nature of their contractionist activities had a perfectly comprehensible rationale. As prudent financiers, and as men with monopoly power over the money supply, they naturally acted to perpetuate their power. Using their dominance of government to dictate to public policy, they contrived to maintain gold, a metal the available stocks of which increased more slowly than population and commercial need, as the single standard of value. The shrinking supply of gold relative to the true monetary needs of society exerted a continual downward pressure upon prices and wages, increased the real value of each existing unit of currency, and worked increasing hardship upon the debtors and taxpaying public. Moreover, the pursuance of gold monometallism with its predictable deflationary effects increased the real yields on the fixed income assets held by the financiers and banking houses, thus rendering ordinarily more rewarding but uncertain speculative investments unnecessary. Financiers controlled the money supply and the government. The government issued bonds, the bonds were acquired by the banking houses, and the banking houses permitted deflation to increase the true value of bond yields. Populists regarded the convergence of these policies as a subtle and pernicious form of extortion practiced upon the debtor majority.[20]

Having identified the enemy and having delineated its methods of operation, Populists undertook to explain how the enemy acquired such terrible and oppressive power. The answer lay in the relationship of the banking community and the venal men who served in positions of public trust, the governmental officials, elective and appointive. Government bond policy in large part suggested this conclusion. Populists called the government-banker relationship "paternalism."[21] Populist contempt for "paternalism" may appear strange, especially since some Populists on some occasions suggested that the government, which, in its unpurified form, they roundly detested, take control of such important elements of the economy as the transportation system and the issuance of currency. But any serious analysis of Populist commentary in Congress points to the inescapable conclusion that Populists were more concerned about the evils of private "ownership" of government than they were in advocating government ownership of segments of the private economy which seemed to be uncontrollable by natural market forces. Belief in competition and a free market were normally compatible with the Populists' deep anti-monopoly instincts, but when circumstances provoked tension between the two, Populists resolved the dilemma by opting for the anti-monopoly position. This was perhaps the basic reason for the ambivalence which inhered in the Populist variant of conservatism.

Paternalism, to the western Populists, not only nurtured and sustained monopoly but also precluded the successful operation of the natural laws of the marketplace. It permitted the few "to control the necessities of the people and to rob them."[22] Any subsidy, any grant, any policy, any evidence of governmental favoritism to any interest group was reprehensible and contradictory to economic law. Anti-paternalism was the fundamental precept of the Populist faith, and it applied equally to farmers, laborers, railroads, industrial corporations and banking houses. It dictated Populist attitudes on social policy and on appropriations for the maintenance of dependent groups such as the Indians, an area in which the Populist mentality hardly stood directly in the rays of enlightened humanitarianism.

The generalized political, social and economic attitudes of the Populists remained basically unchanged from 1891 to 1899, although the particular scope of their activities and the allocation of their energies were frequently determined by the legislation and issues generated by the major parties. On the average, western Populists were active and vocal congressmen; their southern compatriots, on the other hand, were normally mute. In the Fifty-fifth Congress, the last one in which Populists comprised a notable element in federal politics, circumstances necessitated a deemphasis of many original Populist issues such as currency expansion and free silver in favor of concentration on newly prominent issues—Cuba, the Spanish-American War, the Philippines, the problem of war finance, and the subsequent problems of military reorganization and appropriations.

Populist congressmen were active social critics, not responsible and committed legislators. Successful legislation was impossible for them in any case, given their minority position in the Congress, and they normally attempted to avoid superfluous activity. Only in the areas of private relief and pension bills did they function as ordinary congressmen. Nevertheless, as a matter of philosophic necessity, nearly every Populist sponsored a currency expansion bill, usually a silver coinage measure, and watched it die in committee.[23] In the earlier congresses Populists introduced a few measures to curtail the activities of national banks and to reverse federal debt and bond policies.[24] Proposals to reform homestead and irrigation policies, and legislation to pry open Indian reservations to homestead entry, were also commonplace.[25] Legislation dealing with railroad problems, except for the resolution of railroad bond and land grant difficulties, was surprisingly rare.[26] Indeed, western Populists devoted far more time and energy to broader policy questions such as the income tax, the tariff, bond issues, Cuba, and the military establishment as well as to a rigorous and heavy-handed scrutiny of all appropriations matters. Legislative activity with a humane or "liberal" rationale—child labor reform, the eight-hour day, woman suffrage—was exceedingly uncommon in Populist congressional circles.[27]

Undoubtedly the smaller Populist delegations in the earlier congresses were ideologically purer than their fusionist successors of 1896 and certainly more closely attuned to the original agrarian-dissident core of the movement.

Nevertheless, in performance terms there was some continuity, for western Populists from their first appearance in the House used that body as a forum and a pulpit rather than as a potential instrument of reform. And the central concerns of the Populist congressmen – monetary policy, government debt and bond policy, anti-monopoly exhortations – exhibited similar continuity, though circumstances changed considerably. Similarly, Populist demands for appropriations retrenchment grew increasingly indignant from one Congress to the next.[28]

In addition, there was a certain fixed and inflexible assumption which underlay the Populist critique of monopoly-dominated contemporary life. The assumption was that bankers, financiers and other monopolists conducted their activities in contravention of the natural laws of the marketplace system and in violation of the historic American commitment to the competitive free-enterprise ideal. Their opposition to "paternalism" had its roots in philosophic conviction and a particular perception of past (unfortunately bygone) reality. William Alexander Harris of Kansas, for example, broke with the long Democratic tradition of his family because he regarded Populism as more consistent with the traditions of Jefferson and Calhoun than the major parties.[29] More graphically, Harris' Kansas colleague William Baker declared himself to be "internally, externally, and eternally opposed to subsidies" to any group in any form.[30] The subsidized groups, of course, comprised the "merciless, moneyed aristocracy who sought to destroy the liberties of the American people."[31] But perhaps the most impressive damnation of paternalism was uttered by William McKeighan of Nebraska as he eulogized the work ethic and the acquisitive instinct: "the people I represent are not anarchists, they are not opposed to the accumulation of wealth, but they are opposed to its unjust distribution; they believe that the accumulation of wealth is the first step in social improvement and that the next thing in importance is its proper distribution, if left free to follow natural laws, would be found in accordance with the skill, industry and economy of those who toil."[32]

This was the economic world the Populists plaintively recalled and wished to restore – a world of small, individual producers and consumers, each individually endeavoring to buy cheaply and sell dearly, all of them unable and unwilling to resort to collusion or to employ extraneous means to impose their wills upon the marketplace and to contravene its dictates. It was the view from *The Wealth of Nations*. And the key to the depression which beset the nation in the 1890s, in the estimation of Populists, was the money monopoly which clogged the distribution mechanism of the economy. Overproduction theories, sometimes advanced by Republican spokesmen in the 1890s, evoked contemptuous responses from Populists. McKeighan, for example, argued that farmers might indeed restrict output to raise commodity prices, but output restriction carried to its logically absurd conclusion would involve starving their only customers.[33] Populists believed in rigorous expansion; contraction was the policy of the money monopolists who dictated currency, tariff and domestic fiscal policy, the singular method of the paternalists.

The most obvious example of how the money monopolists employed paternalism to guarantee an inequitable distribution of wealth and income was the protective tariff system, although the tariff, in official Populist pronouncements, appeared as a minor, derivative and generally inconsequential issue. It was merely an appendage to the money monopoly. Nevertheless, Populists were obliged to devote considerable attention to this appendage since Congress considered two major tariff proposals during the period of Populist insurgence, the Democratic Wilson bill of 1894 and the Republican Dingley bill of 1897. And on a personal level several Populusts considered the tariff system as more consequential than did the party on an official level.[34] One congressman, in fact, went so far as to declare that punitive retaliation against American protectionism kept American grain from the mouths of "150,000,000 European consumers who never tasted wheat bread."[35]

Essentially, however, Populists disliked the tariff system for three reasons: it represented blatant favoritism, i.e. paternalism; it was an unjust and inequitable revenue-raising method; and it exacerbated an already unnatural distribution of income in the society, and, hence, worked a continual hardship on the toiling masses.[36] One Populist phrased his objections to protectionism with arresting succinctness: "Take down the tariff wall, take off the shackles, and we will take care of ourselves."[37] Many Populists, however, assessed the tariff issue as a sham and an irrelevance since prosperity and depression had occurred under both low tariff and high tariff circumstances. Other factors, primarily monetary, determined economic conditions.[38] The tariff incited Populist wrath because it represented paternalism of the worst kind, it affronted natural economic law, and it was used to divert attention from more basic and consequential issues. Secondly, the tariff promoted resources and income maldistribution and yielded benefits only to its sponsors, the "capitalists, corporations, national banks, rings and trusts...," who comprised, in sum, not more than 25,000 Americans.[39]

But Populists realized the contemporary distribution of power in the United States meant that the tariff would be a permanent fact of life, and they strove principally to identify and mitigate its grossest inequities. This explains their support of the Wilson-Gorman tariff of 1894, which contained a welcome income tax feature, and their thorough condemnation of the

Dingley bill of 1897, which revived the most inequitable elements of the protective system.[40] If protection was really necessary, a number of Populists
argued, it should be equitable protection, protection of small producers
rather than millionaires, and the class legislation elements of the tariff which
impoverished some to enrich others should be abolished.[41]

Most of the Populist tariff analysis occurred in the lengthy debate on the
Dingley bill, a bill which Curtis H. Castle seriously proposed to retitle "a bill
to foster trusts and to pauperize and peonize the agricultural laborers of the
United States."[42] The Dingley measure merited criticism on all of the standard counts. It was inequitable, class-based, inadequate and unfair as a revenue-
raising instrument, inimical to America's future quest for foreign markets,
and stupidly predicated on the assumption that a society could be taxed into
prosperity. Moreover, Populists expressed the conviction that the additional
revenue generated by an increase in tariff rates was unnecessary, that the
people were already taxed beyond their capacity to pay, that government salaries and other expenses should be reduced, and that revenue could be pro-
cured more equitably through the medium of the income tax. The income
tax, which held out some hope of tax equity, was strongly recommended by
the western Populists as an alternative to the tariff. It also possessed a powerful punitive potential, and Populists undoubtedly relished the thought of pre-
senting the nine per cent of the American public who owned 71 per cent of
the nation's wealth with a sizeable bill for past and present exploitation of
the masses.[43] But they had no power to pursue the matter and gave no more
than unanimous intellectual assent to the income tax idea. In any event Populists did not regard taxation as the most significant cause of the current
economic distress and evinced concern about taxes only in the context of
their general insistence upon equity.

To Populists the tariff controversy represented a great evasion of reality.
The issue was money, not tariff rates. In the debate on the Dingley tariff Silver Republican John F. Shafroth of Colorado observed tartly that "the only
issue that is really before the American people is the issue between gold and
silver."[44] In one context or another every articulate Populist congressman
offered a similar assessment. The real issue, in reality the only issue, was
money. And no contemporary of the Populists, and no subsequent student of
the movement, has ever doubted that Populists were consciously dedicated to
the cause of currency inflation and that, in the end, they came to the conclusion that the restoration of the unlimited coinage of silver, i.e. "free silver,"
offered the most convenient and likely means to achieve this inflation. The
other issue, which poses an unanswerable question, was whether the partisans
of gold monometallism were really as intentionally evil, self-centered and

socially pernicious as the Populists believed them to be and as completely dominant in monetary affairs as the Populists claimed.

It has not been so widely recognized, however, that Populists regarded silver as only one acceptable inflationary instrument. Perhaps a majority of Populists accepted silver as the best device, but it was only one mechanism among many. It is even less widely recognized that Populists were not "irresponsible" inflationists. In fact, there were some inflationary proposals which they strenuously opposed, and the basic reasons for their favorable attitude toward the idea of inflation have often been misunderstood. That debtor interests in the United States and elsewhere have exhibited a demonstrable historical attraction to inflationary panaceas — "cheap" money, "soft" money or merely more money — is a commonplace truism, but Populist inclination toward free silver was more philosophically rooted and more social in its rationale than most inflationary proposals of the past. Having identified chronic and deliberately perpetrated currency shortage as the efficacious cause of economic depression in the 1890s, Populists thoroughly believed that currency expansion, through silver coinage or some other respectable medium, would not only raise prices and alleviate the impoverishment of their debtor constituents but would also generate a formidable expansion of overall economic activity with positive and salutary effects on all individuals and institutions, public and private.[45]

Money, in Populist thought, was the key to economic expansion and to the resolution of the depression of the 1890s. Money served no other purpose than as an instrument to facilitate exchange. "Man is a trading animal," alleged Jerry Simpson, and he needed a common denominator to facilitate his trading activities.[46] More money produced more exchange, and more exchange generated more productivity and induced prosperity. Only in this broad social context did silver, the venerable "dollar of the daddies," acquire true importance. Nevertheless, while nearly every Populist introduced a silver coinage bill at one time or another during his congressional tenure, the primary use to which Populists put the silver coinage issue was the negative one of demonstrating that the denial of the free coinage of silver had caused and prolonged the current economic stagnation. Hence silver arguments were almost always offered in the context of debate on other issues rather than submitted to Congress in isolation from other concerns. In fact Populist advocacy of silver reached its peak in Congress rather early, in the context of the debates of 1893 on repeal of the Sherman Silver Purchase Act. Their subsequent efforts on behalf of the metal were considerably more restrained.[47]

Thus western Populists devoted less specific effort to the cause of silver coinage than the prominence of the issue would seem to suggest. And, while

Populists were admitted and unabashed inflationists, they did not favor currency inflation at any price or by any device. The so-called sub-treasury system proposed in the Omaha Platform of the People's Party, a scheme to create circulating media on the security of staple crops deposited in government warehouses, elicited no support from congressional Populists even though the idea was basic to the party's fundamental testament, the Omaha Platform.[48] More importantly, however, Populists opposed a bill proposed in the Fifty-third Congress to repeal the ten per cent tax on the note issues of state banks, a tax enacted in the 1860s as an amendment to the National Banking Act and designed to eliminate the state bank notes from the nation's circulating media. The repeal bill, favored only by William Baker in the Populist delegation, was an obvious inflationary move, but Populists considered it senseless, irresponsible, inferior to silver or greenbacks, and "another miserable makeshift."[49] Repeal, argued the Populists, would surely increase the supply of currency, but it would also engender confusion and uncertainty among the people, offer new opportunities for disreputable corporate elements, and promote the use of state notes for local purposes while encouraging the hoarding of legitimate legal tender. In sum, repeal would allow "44 different states to issue 44 kinds of wildcat currency under 44 different laws," an unseemly recapitulation upon the days of the wildcat banks.[50] John C. Bell of Colorado provided an apt summary of Populist thought on the matter when he argued that the astute course for the nation would be to promote "money, not bank convenience; encourage thrift, not sloth; aid the money user, not the money hoarder; make money more profitable to use in the developing of the enterprises of the country, instead of giving a premium to the man who holds his money for hire...."[51]

After 1896, however, Populists realized that the cause of monetary inflation through silver or federal treasury note issues enjoyed little prospect of success. While they never gave up on silver, they did undertake to explore other avenues of currency expansion and also endeavored to prevent further diminution of the money supply. In 1898, for example, the House entertained a proposal to abolish the century-old practice of governmental assumption of the costs of transporting gold bullion from the smelting plants to the mint. This practice, of course, constituted a subsidy to gold producers, but Populists roundly denounced the bill, arguing that it would increase costs for the mining firms, decrease profits and hinder production, and in the end yield a further decrease in the nation's supply of circulating media. Populist support of this *de facto* subsidy practice was unique, but ideological purity was sacrificed in this instance to secure a greater good, i.e., to prevent further contraction of the money supply.[52] Populists never disliked gold as gold; their hatred of gold monometallism was inspired by the intrinsically limited availability of the metal and its deflationary effects. Secondly, in order to stimulate an increase in gold coinage Populists also advocated that the government coin the seignorage, that is, the small amounts of gold retained by the Treasury from the bullion supplies brought to the mint for coinage as the government's fee for providing the minting service.[53] In these minor ways, therefore, Populists in the twilight of their tenure in the House managed to accommodate themselves to gold and to serve the cause of its expanded circulation and use.

There was one point in the politico-economic analysis of the contemporary world offered by the Populists in which all of their diffuse concerns—money, prices, tariffs, banking practices, paternalism—truly converged and afforded the best concrete illustration of the innate conservatism of their social attitudes. This was the matter of debt, or more accurately, of federal bond policy. As men elected by and identified with a debtor public Populist congressmen stood in uniform horror of debt. Federal bond policy, which Populists considered to be an instance of contrived, manipulated, deliberate and unnecessary indebtedness, evoked Populist condemnation as rank economic heresy. Twice in the 1890s Populists confronted and did battle with federal bond schemes—once in the Cleveland administration when the gold outflow occasioned by the worsening depression depleted the Treasury's legal reserve and obliged the government to float gold bonds in Europe to replenish its reserve, and again in 1898 in the context of the revenue proposals to finance the war with Spain. The first encounter was muted, owing to the diminished Populist representation in Congress in 1894-1895, the national crisis, and the legal nature of the gold reserve to be replenished,[54] but the second provoked a forthright and belligerent response from Populists and revealed the philosophical rudiments of their convictions.

To recapitulate, Populists linked all of the problems of the depressed 1890s to a deliberately induced "money famine" engendered by Anglo-American bankers who controlled the money supply and sustained by the paternalistic relationship of the financiers and government. Since the money monopolists controlled the United States Populists were dismayed but not surprised by the McKinley administration's plans to finance the war effort against Spain by a bond issue rather than through the taxation or treasury note mechanisms. In the debate which ensued in Congress on the war revenue proposal almost every Populist present in the Fifty-fifth Congress arose to castigate the measure, thus providing a convenient and capsule statement of the Populist faith. Jerry Simpson was distressed that "a short war against a weak opponent" should require deficit financing on a large scale. If the government had pursued sensible policies such as silver coinage and progressive income taxation the economy would have benefited enormously and the war effort could be financed from ordinary revenues, he alleged.[55] A bond issue would impose an unjust burden upon present and future generations of taxpayers, and Americans already groaned under the weight of the exactions imposed by public authorities and the money monopoly. A bond issue merely served the greed of financiers whose banking houses and wealthy clients could hardly forego a lucrative, safe and tax-free opportunity.[56]

In an incisive appraisal of the bond proposal Jeremiah Botkin of Kansas discerned three unwarranted benefits which it conferred upon the financial interests. It offered a convenient investment, a means to expand the activities of the National Banks since the note issues of these banks were tied to the volume of bonds in their portfolios, and an undeniable opportunity to commit the nation irrevocably to the gold standard by deflecting pressures to finance the war through treasury note issues or other inflationist devices. Ultimately, he charged, the bonds would be redeemed by exactions on the working people, and, to exacerbate the situation further, the government would be induced to run budget surpluses in order to amortize its debt and thus to contract the available currency supply even more sharply.[57] Hence the net effect of the bond mechanism duplicated the tariff by guaranteeing inequities in the distribution of income, inequities which in the case of bonds might be transmitted to future generations. To the Populists income taxation and any reasonable form of currency inflation were preferable to bond issues as instruments to secure adequate revenues for the military emergency.[58] William L. Greene of Nebraska asserted that the bond proposals emanated from "the hook-nosed Jews of Wall Street" who had cornered the gold market.[59] But ethnic disparagement was infrequent in the Populist critique, and a class-rooted analysis of the bond schemes afforded more compelling and impressive conclusions. The arguments against bonds offered by the Populists in the debate of 1898 resembled those previously used against the protective tariff. Hence the bond measure was condemned as unnecessary, as unjustly burdensome to ordinary taxpayers, as monetarily contractionist, as maldistributive of income, as an inferior revenue instrument, as contrary to economic law, as an unbusinesslike fiscal practice, and as morally wrongful and oppressive.[60] In the context of military necessity, John E. Kelley of South Dakota thought the plutocrats should welcome income taxation as an appealing way to demonstrate their patriotism![61] The financial aspects of the war policy disturbed him to the point that he wondered aloud "shall we free the Cubans by enslaving our own children?"[62]

Thus the bond proposal of 1898, which was generally implemented, tied financial policy to the problems of foreign policy and necessarily added a new dimension to Populist concerns. Populist congressmen, commencing with the emergence of the Cuban issue in 1895, involved themselves in the foreign policy debates of the last half of the decade, in the war with Spain, and in the subsequent problems of the American presence in the Philippines. With few exceptions the Populists were sympathetic to expansionism and to the imperial ideal, both for reasons of humanitarianism and market expansion, though not long after they cast their votes for the war resolution in 1898 many of them developed qualms about their previous conduct.[63]

Their reservations were in part induced by the bond scheme, in part by the conviction that financial interests were using the war for their own purposes, and in part by the belated realization that imperialism entailed great costs for American society and offered ordinary men only symbolic rewards. Empire, Populists suddenly comprehended, required a colonial bureaucracy and an expanded military apparatus, the costs of which would necessarily be borne by the producing classes of America.[64] Some Populists even questioned the prudence of freeing Cuba from its Spanish overlords. Freed from the exactions of Spanish taxgatherers, would the defenseless Cubans ultimately be exploited more thoroughly by the Americans as agents of the money power extended their activities to the island?[65] Was the insurrectionary response of the Filipinos to their benevolent new masters a harbinger of a future reality of broader proportions?[66] Populists, however briefly, were among the first to be distressed by and to speculate about the darker side of imperialism.

It is obvious that the cast of Populist thought was overwhelmingly economic, markedly defensive, and centered upon issues of money and the incidence of cost. In no area of policy did Populists grow more indignant, or demonstrate their conservatism so clearly, as in the related matters of governmental appropriations and costs. Almost without exception the Populist approach to public spending was that of the meat-axe. Government, seemingly by definition, was guilty of inefficiency and excess. To sophisticated Americans two generations subsequent to the Populists their penuriousness must seem amusing and quaint. But, professing that "retrenchment should be the order of the day,"[67] Populists from the beginning to the end of their congressional presence normally voted in the negative on appropriations bills. Among their most remarkable idiosyncracies was the conviction that the salaries of elective and appointive public officers should be reduced.[68] (Salary reduction was also a standard demand of Populists in state government and a part of the platforms of state Populist parties.) The only significant exception to their retrenchment propensities occurred in the context of private pension bills, an area in which Populists, with some exceptions, behaved like other politicians beholden to a constituency with numerous aged, infirm, and military veteran members.

Three aspects of governmental appropriations, the military, the District of Columbia, and the Post Office Department, were particularly evocative of Populist indignation. Until 1898 military appropriations represented a normally dormant issue, but the annual matter of funds to operate the military academy at West Point constituted a significant exception. West Point, with the elitism implicit in its image, received distressingly favorable treatment at appropriations time according to Populists like Lafayette Pence and John Grant Otis. Otis once suggested that the academy's costs might be reduced if the carpeting in the House chamber could be cut up at the conclusion of each session and sent to West Point for use as saddle blankets![69] But in reality the great struggle over military appropriations occurred in 1898 and 1899 coincident with the war and the beginnings of insurrection against American rule in the Philippines. The McKinley administration proposed to increase the size of the standing army to 100,000 men from its traditional 26,500 and to reform and streamline army organization.

Populists reacted vehemently to the army reorganization plan, partly on the basis of cost and partly because of the purportedly deleterious social consequences. They speculated that this enlarged force might well be employed to quell strikes and other forms of domestic political and social unrest.[70] At the same time they observed that a large permanent army had historically been associated with the centralization of governmental and administrative machinery characteristic of imperialist societies. Thus army reorganization affronted the Populist belief in atomic social relationships and a government of minimum scope and power. Furthermore, the logistical needs of an expanded military apparatus afforded innumerable opportunities for new collusive arrangements between the corporate powers and the public authority, and some Populists predicted the emergence of a nascent "military-industrial complex" closely tied to the financial community.[71] More immediately of concern, however, were the new burdens which military expansion imposed directly upon the taxpaying public. To soften this impact Populists subjected the McKinley administration's army reorganization and appropriations proposals of 1898 and 1899 to scathing and disdainful analysis. They opposed the proposed increase in the number of army clerks, the provisions for quartering officers, especially in "expensive" hotels, the assignment of superfluous officers to sinecures in the nation's colleges as professors of "military science," the collusive arrangements between the government and the railroads on the costs of troop transport, and the opportunities which army expansion offered to the "parasite class to enforce commercialism and militarism," most of which was uneconomic in nature.[72] One congressman closely aligned with the Populists thought that the expenditure of $22,000,000 in the Philippines to secure a $10,000,000 trade constituted indefensible business practice.[73] A far better alternative to army expansion, in the estimation of Populists, was the maintenance of a small army and a large National Guard, the latter comprised of men resident and loyal to their home communities.[74] Otherwise, asserted Curtis Castle of California, "the men whose grimy hands feed and clothe this army are the only ones in this land to be crushed and broken by it."[75] But again this outpouring of Populist venom availed nothing.

Populists also singled out the financing and operation of the District of Columbia as a conspicuous fiscal inequity imposed upon the taxpayers of the states. The costs of government and services in the District were met by its local residents and the American public in equal proportions, and Populists scrutinized every aspect of local expenditure proposals. Even so minor a measure as a street improvement bill drew criticism as a contrivance of Washington real estate speculators intent upon improving the value of their properties at public expense.[76] And payment of half of the city's tax bill by the general public, in spite of the fact that the federal government owned at least half of the local real property, appeared to Populist congressmen as an "outrage."[77] Moreover, Populists alleged that local appropriations reflected indefensible padding, and it appeared absurd to one congressman that Washington, comparable in size to Milwaukee, should require three times as many policemen.[78]

The denial of local self-government to the residents of the District of Columbia also prompted considerable Populist criticism. Freeman Knowles of Nebraska, for example, pointedly asked if residents of the capitol area were less capable of exercising their full civil rights than other Americans and if the presence of large numbers of black people in the District constituted a subtle and unmentionable rationale for the retardation of home rule. If this was indeed the case, Knowles thought it was completely senseless. "If you turn the government of this district over to the niggers they could not possibly establish a government as corrupt as the present one," he charged.[79]

Another area of appropriations which evoked the wrath of western Populists was the United States Post Office Department, a public facility which Populists alleged was replete with corruption in its operations and afforded gross examples of paternalism in its policies. Populists never advocated the removal of the postal service from the public sector, but they did contend that most postal appropriations comprised "subsidies" rather than prudent and legitimate disbursements of public funds. They were particularly incensed by the presumed collusive arrangements made between the government and the railroads, arrangements which provided numerous "extra allowances" for carrying mail by rail and which resulted in a carrying rate of three to seven times greater than rates assessed by express companies for providing the same services.[80] Secondly, some Populists claimed that railroads padded weights in the mail cars and thereby extorted an "uncalled for, unwarranted and needless subsidy" from the public purse.[81] The Populist attack on the post office climaxed in the 1898 session of Congress. Some Populists recommended that the government acquire and operate its own mail cars, while others, with notable lack of success, undertook to amend the postal appropriations bill to guarantee that railroads were forbidden to assess the government more for the carrying of mail than they charged private customers for providing similar services.[82] To the ever loquacious Curtis Castle of California the entire postal episode reflected another instance of the "miserly economy of the government in its transactions with the poor and the munificent liberality when dealing with rich corporations" which meant, in sum, that "monopoly owns the Executive Department."[83]

In addition, the McKinley administration, citing a considerable postal deficit, sought to increase the rates on second-class mail from 1 cent per pound to 8 cents per pound. Populists interpreted this to be a covert attempt at censorship of the rural press, which enjoyed second-class mailing privileges, by making the circulation of the country weeklies economically unfeasible. Alleging that the rural press "helps to democratize America" a number of Populist congressmen saw the rate change as an effort to suppress a part of the media which subjected the administration to constant criticism. Needless to say, the increase would also afford the railroads an opportunity to effect an increase in their mail carrying subsidies.[84]

Certain easily identifiable themes were constant in the voluminous Populist criticism of appropriations measures. The subsidy principle violated "the law of competition, the law of self-preservation."[85] Government officials failed to "apply in the administration of the public business the same care, common sense and honesty we apply in private business."[86] Or, similarly, "public servants ought to handle the money of the people with the same care as we would handle our own."[87] Or, stated another way, "in the appropriation and expenditure of public money equal and exact justice should be the underlying principle."[88]

The theme was forthright and simple: equity, equal and exact justice, the abolition of paternalistic practices. In a practical sense the recommendations made by Populists were these: cut costs, cut services, cut taxes, cut public payrolls, eliminate subsidies, eliminate collusion, eliminate paternalism in government-private sector transactions. Essentially the Populist approach was negative, more oriented to the prevention of abuses than to inducing salutary and constructive change. Through all of the Populist criticism and commentary there is detectable a deep strain of faith in pure competition, in laissez-faire, in natural economic law, in the efficacy of the system if its monopolistic clogs could be eliminated and the old competitive practices of small, individually powerless buyers and sellers restored.

Given their demonstrated interest in general questions of policy and governmental procedure, Populist congressmen had little time, and apparently little inclination, for promoting the specific causes of agrarian or labor interest groups. Populist philosophy precluded this kind of activity in any event, for the elimination of paternalistic practices and policies which favored the plutocracy did not mean the inception of equally paternalistic practices and policies on behalf of the producing classes. Indeed, in Congress the original Populist trinity of land, transportation and money congealed into the unity of money. Except in the infrequent debates on railroad mail subsidies and the disposition of railroad bonds held by the federal government Populists rarely addressed themselves to the railroad problem.[89] The contrast between congressional Populism and agrarian-laborite dissidence at the state level was marked on the railroad question, though Jerry Simpson once suggested half-heartedly in the House that the government might perform a useful service if it acquired and operated the rail system.[90]

Populists were somewhat more active on land policy issues, especially on questions of federal involvement in irrigation research and on matters pertaining to the principle of free homesteads. They believed in the maximum availability of the public domain to small farmers and resisted the movement to insulate some lands from private encroachment. For example, Populists opposed the Cleveland administration's removal of lands in the western states from the public domain and designating them as forest reserves, preferring instead to permit the homesteading of forested tracts.[91] In addition, Populists demanded the diminution of Indian reservations to provide more land for homestead entry.[92] Realizing that attractive arable land was in short supply, the western Populists expressed great concern that America would eventually become a society of landless individuals. To Edwin Ridgely of Kansas the prospects for the nation were bleak indeed. "A homeless citizenship," he observed, "means a dying government and a dying civilization."[93] Yet Populists never really came to grips with land policy, and after brief encounters with the issues of homesteads, forest reserves and irrigation they directed their energies toward other problems.

It is obvious that all of the central themes of congressional Populism were grossly economic. For the more qualitative aspects of social policy, such as the conditions of racial and ethnic minorities in America, they exhibited disinterest or disdain. On the few occasions in which they addressed themselves to Indian policy, for example, their attitudes were uncompromisingly reactionary. They spoke in favor of diminishing the land area of the reservations both in the states and in Oklahoma Territory and the opening of these areas to homestead entry and they opposed appropriations for Indian education, especially for the Carlisle Indian School in Pennsylvania.[94] Congressman John Grant Otis of Kansas, a birthright Quaker, contended that he had learned on the plains that "Hiawatha and Minnehaha were creatures of fiction, and that the dirty degraded squaw and the poor, cruel, brutal Indian were very different creatures," manageable and educable only in the reservation context.[95] The cynicism reflected in this posture was mitigated only by two instances in which individual Populists supported the Indian cause in litigation emanating from disputed allotments or land claims.[96] Similarly, Populists favored Chinese exclusion and general immigration restriction, largely upon racial and ethnic grounds.[97] John Grant Otis spoke derisively of "the Democratic vote, the ignorant foreign vote," which interfered with the activities of "the educated thinking people of the party, the true reformers."[98] These expressions of disdain for racial and ethnic minorities were intelligible and understandable from the Populist point of view. Populists professed to represent not the dispossessed and unproductive minorities, but the distressed, dispossessed and productive majority!

In monetary and fiscal affairs Populist congressmen, given their assumptions, offered an intelligent and rational critique of the structure and operations of the American economy, and surely their unabashedly instrumentalist conception of money was anticipatory of future attitudes and policy. Undoubtedly their estimate of the effective incidence of collusion and paternalism in the system was overstated, and in any case their efforts to terminate these abuses were marked by futility and frustration. It is hardly possible to examine the performance and commentary of Populist congressmen without being struck by the depth of their commitment to traditional, hoary, conservative values—to a free market, to competition, to a neutral government, to equity, to equal access to resources and institutions, to the work ethic, to the conviction that all men shared an equal obligation to produce and to justify their existence as men. Populists were nineteenth century men in their values and assumptions, not precursors of the fiscal liberalism, the welfare philosophy and the statist orientation of twentieth-century liberal reformers. When they found themselves in need of economic authorities upon whom to rely they chose Adam Smith and David Ricardo, not Richard T. Ely or the other young, reformist American economists who had been trained in the postulates of the German historical school and influenced by the precepts of the *Verein für Sozialpolitik*. Populists, with a few exceptions, readily accepted the reality of the industrial state, but they responded negatively to the attendant corruption and to the surreptitious efforts of special interests to extract special advantages from its fabric.[99] Perhaps they did not appraise the reality of the new industrial state and the complexity of its interest groups with great astuteness and sophistication, for the moral and ethical components of their attitudes sometimes blinded them to the harder realities of economic relationships. They believed in an older order, a world of self-regulating, not selfishly manipulated, mechanisms and processes.

But they soon learned to accept the new order, and not a few of them were ultimately coopted by it. The duration of their reform proclivities was attenuated, and even in the Fifty-fifth Congress a growing ambivalence toward the potential of reform characterized their activities and led them to concentrate on more petty and peevish issues. A recent scholar has observed that the level of Populist militancy was "inversely proportional to the price of leading farm commodities," but this view is surely too simple and too cynical.[100] Yet prices did improve after 1896, militancy did shade into ambivalence, and many Populists began to fraternize with, and ultimately embraced, the enemy. Lafayette Pence became a railroad attorney in New York, for example, and Omer Kem went into public utilities in Oregon. Others entered the service of corporations or relapsed into silence. An old Populist carrying a Progressive banner a decade after 1896 was a distinct rarity.[101] The true Populists were militant old farmers and mining state laborites who died before the turn of the century.

FOOTNOTES TO TEXT

CHAPTER ONE: Western Populism: Postulates and Perspectives

1. The most prominent "revisionist" assessments of Populism are: Richard Hofstadter, *The Age of Reform; from Bryan to F.D.R.* (New York, 1955), 60-93; Oscar Handlin, "American Views of the Jews at the Opening of the Twentieth Century," *Publications of the American Jewish Historical Society*, XL (June, 1951), 323-344; the contributions of Peter Viereck, Talcott Parsons, Seymour Martin Lipset, David Riesman, Nathan Glazer and Richard Hofstadter in Daniel Bell (ed.), *The New American Right* (New York, 1955); Victor C. Ferkiss, "Populist Influences on American Fascism," *Western Political Quarterly*, X (June, 1957), 350-373. An able annotation of this and related literature appears in Walter T. K. Nugent, *The Tolerant Populists; Kansas Populism and Nativism* (Chicago, 1963), 3-27; see also Theodore Saloutos, "The Professors and the Populists," *Agricultural History*, XL (October, 1966), 235-254.

2. Ferkiss, "Populist Influences on American Fascism," 352-359.

3. The most noted of the "counterrevisionist" studies are: Norman Pollack, *The Populist Response to Industrial America* (Cambridge, Mass., 1962); Pollack (ed.), *The Populist Mind* (Indianapolis, 1967), xix-xlviii; Nugent, *The Tolerant Populists*; C. Vann Woodward, "The Populist Heritage and the Intellectual," *American Scholar*, XXIX (Winter, 1959-1960), 55-73; Paul S. Holbo, "Wheat or What? Populism and American Fascism," *Western Political Quarterly*, XIV (September, 1961), 727-736; Martin Ridge, *Ignatius Donnelly: Portrait of a Politician* (Chicago, 1962).

4. Ferkiss, "Populist Influences on American Fascism," 352-359; Pollack, "Fear of Man: Populism, Authoritarianism and the Historian," *Agricultural History*, XXXIX (April, 1965), 67.

5. *Agricultural History*, XXXIX (April, 1965), 59-85. The contributors were Norman Pollack, Irwin Unger, Oscar Handlin and J. Rogers Hollingsworth.

6. George C. Wallace, George McGovern, Hubert H. Humphrey and Senator Fred Harris of Oklahoma were all described, in one context or another, as "populists" during the years 1971 and 1972.

7. The evidence assembled in this study has been culled from the record of the Populist experience in the plains and mountain states, the only areas in which Populists acquired a measure of real power. Hence the South, a region in which the Populist insurgents remained a distinct minority, has not been treated. Nevertheless, there is substantial evidence that southern Populism was at least as conservative as the western variant of the movement, and the author would contend that exclusion of the southern Populist experience does not impair the validity of the arguments presented in this study. See, for

example, the excellent study by Sheldon Hackney, *Populism to Progressivism in Alabama* (Princeton, 1969), especially 71-76, 326-328; and Roscoe C. Martin, *The People's Party in Texas* (Austin, 1933), 52-53, 74, 215, 218.

8. These points have been admirably established in three excellent recent studies. See Paul Kleppner, *The Cross of Culture: A Social Analysis of Midwestern Politics, 1850-1900* (New York, 1970), 269-375; Richard J. Jensen, *The Winning of the Midwest; Social and Political Conflict, 1888-1896* (Chicago, 1971), 209-237, 269-308; and Samuel T. McSeveney, *The Politics of Depression; Political Behavior in the Northeast, 1893-1896* (New York, 1972), 3-31, 163-229. [Author's note: The reference to the reformed and reconstituted character of the Republican party should not be construed to mean that the Republican establishment was devoid of conservatives. To the critical reader such names as Chauncey Depew, Nelson Aldrich, Joseph G. Cannon, William Boyd Allison and many others will immediately come to mind. These individuals, however, were members of a very different conservative genre than the Populists, and they were quite congenially attuned to the corporate and institutional reality of industrial America.]

9. See Resolution 9, Omaha Platform of the People's Party of America, July 4, 1892, reproduced in John D. Hicks, *The Populist Revolt* (Minneapolis, 1931), 444.

10. John R. Rogers, *Free Land; the Remedy for Involuntary Poverty, Social Unrest and the Woes of Labor* (Tacoma, Wash., 1897), 12; Rogers, *The Inalienable Rights of Man* (Olympia, Wash., 1900), 11; *Congressional Record*, 53 Cong., 1 Sess., Appendix, 289-300, 339-340 (October 7, 11, 1893); *Congressional Record*, 53 Cong., 3 Sess., 977 (January 15, 1895).

11. John D. Hicks, "The Sub-Treasury: A Forgotten Plan for the Relief of Agriculture," *Mississippi Valley Historical Review*, XV (December, 1928), 355-373.

12. *Congressional Record*, 53 Cong., 1 Sess., Appendix, 289-340 (October 7, 11, 1893) (address by William Vincent Allen of Nebraska); Wichita *Kansas Commoner*, September 24, 1891; Davis H. Waite, undated (1892) address, copy in Waite Papers, Colorado State Archives.

13. See Resolution 2 of the Omaha Platform, reproduced in Hicks, *The Populist Revolt*, 443; *Congressional Record*, 53 Cong., 2 Sess., 1079 (January 19, 1894).

14. Most Populists were mute on this point. In his prodigious study, *The Roots of the Modern American Empire* (New York, 1969), William Appleman Williams included Populists among the "farm businessmen" whose quest for foreign markets comprised, in his view, the taproot of American imperialism. But he correctly observed that Populists were neither in the vanguard of agricultural expansionism nor atypical of "farm businessmen" as an interest group. Furthermore, his analysis of Populist interest in expanded foreign markets relied largely upon the commentary of William Vincent Allen and, to a lesser extent, Jerry Simpson. Allen was not a representative Populist figure and Simpson, who quickly concluded that market expansion presaged imperialism and war, reverted to a primary emphasis on domestic policy and eventually condemned imperialism. See Williams, *The Roots of the Modern American Empire*, 347-348, 363-364, 374-375, 386, 415, 420, 426.

15. Sidney Fine, *Laissez-faire and the General Welfare State* (Ann Arbor, 1956), 3-25, 47-67, 112-113.

16. *Congressional Record*, 53 Cong., 1 Sess., 776 (August 23, 1893); 54 Cong., 1 Sess., 36-37, 294, 1448-1449 (December 4, 24, 1895; February 7, 1896); 55 Cong., 2 Sess. 39-40, (December 8, 1897). In Kansas, Populist governor John W. Leedy also equated the free coinage of silver with the penetration of markets in Latin America. See Topeka *Daily Capital*, April 4, 1897; Topeka *Advocate*, April 4, 1897.

17. *Ibid.*, 55 Cong., 2 Sess., 3821 (April 13, 1898).

18. Wichita *Kansas Commoner*, September 24, 1891.

19. See chap. 6 below.

20. See chaps. 4 and 5 below.

21. Governor's Message, *Kansas House Journal, 1897* (Topeka, 1897), 12.

22. See references to Washington and Kansas in chap. 6 below. Another excellent example of the penurious nature of Populists and their preference for cheap, sudden and dramatic solutions occurred in the state legislative sessions of 1897. While Populist congressmen were haranguing their colleagues in Washington on America's duty to liberate the oppressed population of Cuba from their Spanish masters, the Populist governors of Nebraska and South Dakota protested against the collection of money for Cuban relief by the Red Cross in their states. A simple declaration in favor of Cuban independence by the United States, they reasoned, would be sufficient to resolve the Cuban issue. See Williams, *The Roots of the Modern American Empire*, 422-423.

23. Rogers, *Free Land*, 10.

24. These arguments were advanced in a number of Rogers' pamphlets. See especially *Free Land* (1897); *The Inalienable Rights of Man* (1900); and *Homes for the Homeless* (Seattle, 1895). See also Russell Blankenship, "The Political Thought of John R. Rogers," *Pacific Northwest Quarterly*, XXXVII (January, 1946), 3-13.

25. Capable analyses of the mugwumps and their attitudes are: John G. Sproat, *The "Best Men"; Liberal Reformers in the Gilded Age* (New York, 1968), especially 112-141, 272-281; Hofstadter, *The Age of Reform*, 134-143; Geoffrey Blodgett, "Reform Thought and the Genteel Tradition," in H. Wayne Morgan (ed.), *The Gilded Age* (2nd ed.; Syracuse, 1970), 55-76.

26. David P. Thelen, *The New Citizenship; Origins of Progressivism in Wisconsin, 1885-1900* (Columbia, Mo., 1972), 49, 69, 137, 150-151, 152, 161-165, 211, 225, 237.

27. William Vincent Allen was the most forceful Populist spokesman for a community of interest of West and South through the auspices of the People's Party.

28. The reference is to the election of William Alexander Harris to the House of Representatives. Harris was elected *at large*.

29. The importance of legitimacy in a society with revolutionary origins is explored in Michael Kammen, *People of Paradox; An Inquiry Concerning the Origins of American Civilization* (New York, 1972), especially 49-56, 217-218.

30. Rogers, *Free Land*, 12; *Homes for the Homeless*, 30-40; see also Margaret Hollinshead Thompson, "The Writings of John Rankin Rogers" (MA Thesis, University of Washington, 1948), 74-78; the quotation appears in *The Inalienable Rights of Man*, 25.

31. The later careers of Jerry Simpson, William Vincent Allen, Lorenzo Lewelling, Davis Waite and a number of Populist congressmen are instructive in this regard.

32. Lawrence C. Goodwyn, "Populist Dreams and Negro Rights: East Texas as a Case Study," *American Historical Review*, LXXVI (December, 1971), 1435-1456; William M. Chafe, "The Negro and Populism: A Kansas Case Study," *Journal of Southern History*, XXXIV (August, 1968), 402-409; Jack Abramowitz, "The Negro in the Populist Movement," *Journal of Negro History*, XXXVIII (July, 1953), 257-289.

33. Robert H. Wiebe, *The Search for Order, 1877-1920* (New York, 1967), 1-11.

34. Boise *Idaho Daily Statesman*, August 3, 1894.

35. See, in this connection, Samuel Emlen Walker, "Populism and Industrialism: The Ideology of the Official Organ of the Nebraska Populist Movement" (MA Thesis, University of Nebraska, Omaha, 1970), 40, 95-97. Walker's study is an analysis of the Lincoln *Alliance*.

36. The selection of Lewelling and Waite as illustrative of the character of Populist executives represents a deliberate choice which involves the exclusion of such figures as John R. Rogers of Washington and John W. Leedy of Kansas from individualized treatment. Rogers played only a marginal role in the Populist movement, and Leedy was a decidedly secondary figure. See Karel D. Bicha, "John W. Leedy: Continental Commoner," *Alberta Historical Review*, XXII (Summer, 1974), and, by the same author, "Peculiar Populist: An Assessment of John R. Rogers," *Pacific Northwest Quarterly*, LXV (Summer, 1974). Other Populist endorsed governors, Robert B. Smith of Montana, Frank Steunenberg of Idaho, Andrew Lee of South Dakota, and Silas A. Holcomb of Nebraska were "fusionists" with Democratic party antecedents.

CHAPTER TWO: Jerry Simpson: Populist without Principle

1. Gerald W. Johnson, *The Lunatic Fringe* (Philadelphia, 1957), 147.

2. Walter T. K. Nugent, *The Tolerant Populists: Kansas Populism and Nativism* (Chicago, 1963), 76.

3. *Ibid.*, 77.

4. *Ibid.*, 78.

5. Annie L. Diggs, *The Story of Jerry Simpson* (Wichita, 1908), 15-50.

6. *Ibid.*, 54-57.

7. Barber County (Medicine Lodge) *Index*, Oct. 6, Nov. 3, 1886. Unless otherwise indicated, newspaper citations refer to Kansas newspapers. Thomas A. McNeal, *When Kansas was Young* (New York, 1922), 202-204; Myron C. Scott, "A Congressman and His Constituents: Jerry Simpson and the Big Seventh" (MA Thesis, Fort Hays Kansas State College, 1959), Chap. 1.

8. Raymond C. Miller, "The Populist Party in Kansas" (Ph.D. Dissertation, University of Chicago, 1928), 62, 318; Raymond Curtis Miller, "The Background of Populism in Kansas," *Mississippi Valley Historical Review*, XI (March, 1925), 477, 481-83.

9. Miller, "Populist Party in Kansas," 54-55; Anna Rochester, *The Populist Movement in the United States* (New York, 1943), 49-50.

10. Topeka *Kansas Farmer*, Oct. 8, 1890; see also Elizabeth Barr, "The Populist Uprising," in William E. Connelley (ed.), *A Standard History of Kansas and Kansans* (5 vols., Chicago, 1918), II, 1155-65.

11. *Kansas Farmer*, Oct. 8, 1890; Miller, "Populist Party in Kansas," 54-55.

12. Charles K. Franks, "Jerry Simpson—A Kansas Populist" (MA Thesis, Northwestern University, 1940), 21-22; Kansas City (Mo.) *Star*, Jan. 23, 1905.

13. Wichita *Daily Beacon*, Sept. 5, 1890.

14. Henry Clay McDougal, *Recollections, 1844-1909* (Kansas City, Mo., 1910), 152.

15. Emporia *Gazette*, June 28, 1900.

16. Wichita *Daily Eagle*, Nov. 24, 1901.

17. Franks, "Jerry Simpson," iii.

18. "The Political Rebellion in Kansas," in N. A. Dunning (ed.), *The Farmers Alliance History and Agricultural Digest* (Washington, 1891), 280-83; "The Plain People," *Illustrated American*, XXII (Sept. 11, 1897), 332-34; "The Knocker Who Knocks on the Knocker," *Kansas Knocker: A Journal for Cranks*, I (July, 1900), 19-20.

19. The Paper was published from May 8, 1899, to Sept. 17, 1900.

20. Kansas City (Mo.) *Times*, Dec. 16, 1930.

21. Hamlin Garland, "The Alliance Wedge in Congress," *Arena*, V (March, 1892), 447-57; William Allen White, *The Autobiography of William Allen White* (New York, 1946), 217-18.

22. White, *Autobiography*, 217-8.

23. Quoted in Hortense Marie Harrison, "The Populist Delegation in the Fifty-second Congress, 1891-1893" (MA Thesis, University of Kansas, 1933), 18.

24. David D. Leahy, "Vagrant Memories of Fifty Years," El Dorado *Weekly Republican,* Jan. 22, 1915.

25. Barber County *Index,* Oct. 23, 1889.

26. *Ibid.,* Dec. 12, 1894.

27. Wichita *Daily Eagle,,* Oct. 24, 1905.

28. Victor Murdock, *Folks* (New York, 1921), 103.

29. El Dorado *Weekly Republican,* Jan. 22, 1915.

30. *Ibid.*

31. *Ibid.*

32. Harper *Alliance Bulletin,* Sept. 26, 1890.

33. Wichita *Kansas Commoner,* Sept. 24, 1891.

34. Harrison, "Populist Delegation in the Fifty-second Congress," 49-50; Diggs, *Jerry Simpson,* 149.

35. Harper *Alliance Bulletin,* Sept. 26, 1890.

36. *Ibid.*

37. Topeka *Daily Capital,* Jan. 10, 1893; Topeka *State Journal,* Jan. 10, 1893.

38. Diggs, *Jerry Simpson,* 200.

39. *Congressional Record,* 53 Cong., 3 Sess., 3215 (March 2, 1895). In bimetallic theory, "compensatory action" refers to the principle that whenever an increase in the supply of one metal (A) depresses its value in terms of the second metal (B) in the "open market," A will flow into coinage, since the fixed "mint ratio" will favor it. B, in turn, will flow from coinage to the "open market" where it is of greater value in terms of A, but eventually increased supplies of B in the "open market" will depress its value in terms of A on the "open market" and establish a ratio equal to the mint ratio. In effect, holders of metals compensate for divergence of the "market ratio" from the "mint ratio" by selling in the advantageous place, but the cumulative effect, according to partisans of bimetallism, is the equalization of the two ratios and the maintenance in circulation of coins of both metals.

40. Emporia *Gazette,* Dec. 19, 1895.

41. Nugent, *Tolerant Populists,* 188.

42. Wichita *Daily Eagle,* Sept. 27, 1896; Raymond Flory, "The Political Career of Chester I. Long" (Ph.D. Dissertation, University of Kansas, 1955), 9-12.

43. Flory, "Chester I. Long," 11-12; Medicine Lodge *Cresset,* Sept. 18, 1896.

44. Kansas City (Mo.) *Star,* Sept. 14, 1902.

45. Medicine Lodge *Cresset,* May 24, June 7, 1888; Barber County *Index,* May 16, 23, 1888.

46. Medicine Lodge *Cresset,* June 7, 21, 1888.

47. Barber County *Index,* June 6, 1888.

48. Barber County *Democrat,* June 15, 1888.

49. Manchester (N.H.) *Mirror and Farmer,* April 2, 1891.

50. Hallie Farmer, "The Economic Background of Frontier Populism," *Mississippi Valley Historical Review,* X (March, 1924), 426.

51. *Congressional Record,* 53 Cong., 2 Sess., 773 (Jan. 12, 1894).

52. *Kansas Commoner,* Sept. 24, 1891.

53. *Congressional Record,* 52 Cong., 1 Sess., 3108 (April 8, 1892).

54. *Ibid.*

55. *Ibid.,* 3110.

56. *Kansas Commoner*, Sept. 24, 1891.

57. *Ibid.*, Sept. 6, 1894.

58. Wichita *Daily Eagle*, Sept. 27, 1896; Wellington *People's Voice*, Oct. 1, 1896.

59. *Congressional Record*, 52 Cong., 1 Sess., 2131 (April 12, 1892).

60. *Ibid.*, 52 Cong., 2 Sess., 49-50 (Feb. 15, 1893).

61. *Congressional Record*, 55 Cong., 2 Sess., 549 (June 9, 1898); see also *ibid.*, 3821 (April 13, 1898).

62. *Ibid.*, 549 (June 9, 1899); 55 Cong., 3 Sess., 1001-03, 2329 (Jan. 24, Feb. 24, 1899).

63. Barber County *Index*, March 29, April 12, Nov. 1, 1893; see also Medicine Lodge *Cresset*, Sept. 16, 1898.

64. Barber County *Index*, March 10, 1897.

65. Medicine Lodge *Cresset*, July 30, 1897.

66. Barber County *Index*, May 19, 1897.

67. Barr, "Populist Uprising," 1179.

68. Miller, "Populist Party in Kansas," 226; Fred E. Haynes, *James Baird Weaver* (Iowa City, 1919), 346; Topeka *State Journal*, Jan. 19, 23, 1893.

69. Medicine Lodge *Cresset*, Sept. 16, 1897.

70. *Ibid.*, Jan. 21, 1898.

71. *Ibid.*, March 19, 1897; Barber County *Index*, March 17, Dec. 15, 1897.

72. Hutchinson *News*, July 27, 1897.

73. Medicine Lodge *Cresset*, Sept. 3, 1897.

74. *Ibid.*, Sept. 16, 1897, quoting the Topeka *Mail and Breeze*, Sept. 14, 1897.

75. Barber County *Index*, May 25, 1898.

76. Topeka *State Journal*, Jan. 19, 1893; *Jerry Simpson's Bayonet*, May 29, 1899.

77. *Bayonet*, Jan. 8, 1900.

78. *Bayonet*, Jan. 8, 1900; Medicine Lodge *Cresset*, Sept. 16, 1898.

79. *Bayonet*, May 8, 1899; see also Martin Ridge, *Ignatius Donnelly: The Portrait of a Politician* (Chicago, 1962), 128-130, 298-300, 323, 327-328, 342-343, 349, 351, 355, 357, 370.

80. Scott, "A Congressman and His Constituents," 177.

81. Topeka *State Journal*, July 25, 1900.

82. *Ibid.*

83. Topeka *Mail and Breeze*, July 27, 1900.

84. Wichita *Sunday Eagle*, Nov. 11, 1901.

85. "The Knocker Who Knocks on the Knocker," *Kansas Knocker: A Journal for Cranks*, I (July, 1900), 20.

CHAPTER THREE: William Vincent Allen: Misplaced Populist

1. Omaha *Daily Bee*, February 8, 1893.

2. Addison E. Sheldon, "Nebraskans I Have Known: William Vincent Allen," *Nebraska History*, XIX (July, 1938), 200.

3. Quoted in Albert Shaw, "William V. Allen: Populist," *Review of Reviews*, X (July, 1894), 34.

4. Mittie Y. Scott, "The Life and Political Career of William Vincent Allen" (MA Thesis, University of Nebraska, 1927), 3-12.

5. Quoted in *ibid.*, 71.

6. *Ibid.*, 4-12.

7. Sheldon, "Nebraskans I Have Known," 193.

8. Scott, "Life and Political Career of William Vincent Allen," 11.

9. *Ibid., passim*; see also Paolo E. Coletta, "A Tempest in a Teapot? Governor Poynter's Appointment of William V. Allen to the United States Senate," *Nebraska History,* XXXVIII (July, 1957), 155-163.

10. *Ibid.,* 157.

11. *Congressional Record,* 53 Cong., 3 Sess., 974, 980 (January 15, 1895).

12. Shaw, "William V. Allen," 40.

13. Scott, "Life and Political Career of William Vincent Allen," 69.

14. See, for example, Silas Holcomb to Allen, February 18, 1896, Allen Papers, Nebraska Historical Society.

15. Allen to Mrs. J. T. Kellie, February 1, 1894; March 23, 1894; May 7, 1894, Nebraska State Farmers Alliance Papers, Nebraska Historical Society.

16. *Ibid.,* March 23, 1894.

17. *Congressional Record,* 53 Cong., 1 Sess., Appendix, 289-340 (October 7, 11, 1893).

18. *Ibid., passim.*

19. *Ibid.,* 290.

20. *Ibid.*

21. *Ibid.,* 294.

22. *Ibid.,* 290.

23. *Ibid.,* 290-300.

24. *Ibid.*

25. *Ibid.,* 323.

26. *Ibid.,* 339-340.

27. *Ibid.,* 340.

28. William V. Allen, *The Financial Policy* (Washington, 1896), 7, *Congressional Record,* 54 Cong., 1 Sess., Appendix, 310-320 (April 30, 1896).

29. *Congressional Record,* 53 Cong., 1 Sess., Appendix, 330; Allen, *The Financial Policy,* 7-9.

30. Allen, *The Financial Policy,* 2.

31. Shaw, "William V. Allen," 39; Allen, *The Financial Policy,* 11.

32. Madison (Neb.) *Star,* July 31, 1896; see also Shaw, "William V. Allen" 37.

33. *Congressional Record,* 54 Cong., 1 Sess., 1448-1449 (February 8, 1896).

34. *Ibid.;* see also Allen, "Western Feeling Towards the East," *North American Review,* CLXII (May, 1896), 588-593.

35. *Congressional Record,* 53 Cong., 3 Sess., 2022-2036, 2071-2077 (February 11-12, 1895). See also *ibid.,* 428 (December 19, 1894); Sheldon Hackney, *Populism to Progressivism in Alabama* (Princeton, 1969), 49-70.

36. *Congressional Record,* 53 Cong., 3 Sess., 580-581 (January 3, 1895).

37. Allen to Mrs. J. T. Kellie, January 23, 1895. Nebraska Farmers Alliance Papers.

38. Allen, *Cuba Must Be Free* (Washington, 1898), 14.

39. *Congressional Record,* 54 Cong., 1 Sess., 25 (December 3, 1895). *Ibid.,* 2148 (February 27, 1896).

40. Allen, *Cuba Must Be Free,* 9; *Congressional Record,* 54 Cong., 2 Sess., 2172 (February 24, 1897).

41. *Congressional Record,* 54 Cong., 1 Sess., 36-37 (December 4, 1895); 54 Cong., 1 Sess., 294 (December 24, 1895); 54 Cong., 1 Sess., 1448-1449 (February 7, 1896); 55 Cong., 2 Sess., 39-40 (December 8, 1897); 55 Cong., 2 Sess., 4038 (April 18, 1898).

42. Allen, *Cuba Must Be Free,* 12; *Congressional Record,* 55 Cong., 1 Sess., 996 (May 11, 1897).

43. *Congressional Record*, 55 Cong., 3 Sess., 1480-1484, 1491 (February 6, 1899).

44. *Ibid.*, 1737-1738 (February 11, 1899); Allen, "Necessary and Natural Territorial Expansion," in W. J. Bryan (ed.), *Republic or Empire: The Philippine Question* (Chicago, 1899), 304; *Congressional Record*, 55 Cong., 2 Sess., 40 (December 8, 1897).

45. Quoted in Scott, "Life and Political Career of William Vincent Allen," 76.

46. Allen to Mrs. Allen, April 5, 1899. Allen Papers.

47. Allen, "The Necessity for the People's Party," *The Arena*, XXX (October, 1903), 410-414.

48. Sheldon, "Nebraskans I Have Known," 202; Scott, "Life and Political Career of William Vincent Allen," 71 ff.

CHAPTER FOUR: Lorenzo D. Lewelling: Incomplete Humanist

1. Brief biographical sketches of Lewelling, emphasizing his early career, are: Walter J. Costigan, "Lorenzo D. Lewelling," *Transactions of the Kansas State Historical Society*, VII (1901-1902), 121-126 and Dawn Daniels, "Lorenzo D. Lewelling—A Leader of the Kansas Populists" (MA Thesis, Northwestern University, 1931), 1-7.

2. Lewelling to Samuel Limmett, April 20, 1893. Lewelling Papers, Kansas State Historical Society.

3. *Iowa Documents, 1876; Reform School, Report of the Girls Department* (Des Moines, 1876), 49.

4. *Ibid.*, 48.

5. *Ibid.*, *1880*, 58.

6. Lewelling to C. E. Briely, November 14, 1894. Lewelling Papers.

7. Lewelling to J. N. Engall, June 1, 1893. Lewelling Papers.

8. Daniels, "Lorenzo D. Lewelling," 5-7, 17.

9. *Ibid.*, 24-25; see also O. Gene Clanton, *Kansas Populism: Ideas and Men* (Lawrence, 1969), 117, 128.

10. See, for example, his address of July 28, 1894, reprinted in Norman Pollack (ed.), *The Populist Mind* (Indianapolis, 1967), 4-11.

11. Lewelling, "Inaugural Address," reprinted in part as "A Dream of the Future" in Pollack (ed.), *The Populist Mind*, 51-54.

12. Cited in Pollack (ed.), *The Populist Mind*, 5; see also Topeka *Daily Capital*, January 10, 1893 for the full text of the inaugural address.

13. Lewelling, "A Dream of the Future" in Pollack (ed.), *The Populist Mind*, 53.

14. *Ibid.*

15. The most recent account of the "Legislative War" appears in Clanton, *Kansas Populism: Ideas and Men*, 131-139.

16. Lewelling used this expression in his inaugural address. For his legislative recommendations see *Kansas Senate Journal, 1893*, 48-49.

17. Lewelling to Davis H. Waite, December 19, 1894. Waite Papers, Colorado State Archives.

18. *Kansas Senate Journal, 1893*, 48-49.

19. Lewelling to Ben Henderson, April 19, 1893. Lewelling Papers.

20. Lewelling to members of State Board of Public Works (miscellaneous letters), February 18, 1893. Lewelling Papers.

21. Lewelling to W. B. Glasco, June 22, 1893. Lewelling Papers.

22. Lewelling to Mary Elizabeth Lease, December 28, 1893. Lewelling Papers.

23. The unsavory details of this conflict are faithfully related in Clanton, *Kansas Populism: Ideas and Men*, 141-146.

24. Lewelling to Milton E. Phillips, April 8, 1893. Lewelling Papers.

25. Lewelling to Fred J. Close; Lewelling to C. D. Arnold, July 24, 1893. Lewelling Papers.

26. Lewelling to B. D. Waggener, July 9, 1894. Lewelling Papers.

27. Lewelling to J. McLennan, July 26, 1894. Lewelling Papers; *Kansas Public Documents, 1893-1895* (Topeka, 1895), 24.

28. Lewelling Papers for May and June of 1893 contain a large body of letters from constituents demanding a special session of the legislature.

29. W. D. Street to Lewelling and E. R. Bonnefield to Lewelling, April 18, 1893; Joseph Wallace to Lewelling, April 21, 1893; A. S. Cooke to Lewelling, April 21, 1893. Lewelling Papers.

30. Lewelling to G. G. Allen, July 15, 1893. Lewelling Papers.

31. *Ibid.*; Lewelling's negative response to petitions for relief and assistance should be contrasted with the more enlightened and humane reaction of Republican state administrations in the plains region to the deprivation occasioned by the grasshopper infestations of the early 1870s. See Gilbert C. Fite, *The Farmers' Frontier, 1865-1900* (New York, 1966), 55-74.

32. Christ Stegnason to "State Govner," September 3, 1893. Lewelling Papers.

33. J. F. Altaffer to Lewelling, July 1, 1893. Lewelling Papers.

34. County Commissioners of Lane County and Trego County to Lewelling, July 1, 1893, July 17, 1893. Lewelling Papers. Lewelling, like other governors, had no executive budget and was, hence, dependent upon the legislature for funds.

35. Lewelling to Robert Nesbit, May 10, 1894. Lewelling Papers.

36. Lewelling to Police Commissioners of Atchison, December 19, 1893. Lewelling Papers.

37. The "Tramp Circular" appears in full in Costigan, "Lorenzo D. Lewelling," 125-126 and more conveniently in Pollack (ed.), *The Populist Mind*, 330-332.

38. All of the quoted material above appears in the Tramp Circular's text.

39. James L. Switzer to Lewelling, December 9, 1893. Lewelling Papers.

40. George M. Dickson to Lewelling, December 7, 1893; J. G. Thayer to Lewelling, December 7, 1893; J. Bamberger to Lewelling, December 9, 1893. Lewelling Papers.

41. It should be pointed out in this context that Lewelling did appoint blacks to state positions, in contrast to normal Kansas practice, and that on one occasion he detailed state militiamen to Salina to prevent the lynching of a black prisoner. See William H. Chafe, "The Negro and Populism: A Kansas State Study," *Journal of Southern History*, XXXIV (August, 1968), 404, 406, 411, 413, 416, 418.

42. See Clanton, *Kansas Populism: Ideas and Men*, 223.

43. *Ibid.*, 224.

44. Quoted in Daniels, "Lorenzo D. Lewelling," 66, citing Wichita *Eagle*, September 5, 1900.

CHAPTER FIVE: Davis Hanson Waite: The Left Wing

1. Leon W. Fuller, "The Populist Regime in Colorado" (Ph.D. Dissertation, University of Wisconsin, 1933), 6-33; Joel F. Vaile, "Colorado's Experiment with Populism," *The Forum*, XVIII (February, 1895), 714-723. Other studies which demonstrate the labor orientation of mountain state populism are: Thomas A. Clinch, *Urban Populism and Free Silver in Montana* (Missoula, 1970); William J. Gaboury, "Dissension in the Rockies: A History of Idaho Populism" (Ph.D. Dissertation, University of Idaho, 1966); and David B. Griffiths, "Populism in the Far West: 1800-1900" (Ph.D. Dissertation, University of Washington, 1967).

2. Fuller, "Populist Regime in Colorado," 6-40.

3. *Ibid.*, 313.

4. Vaile, "Colorado's Experiment with Populism," 715.

5. Waite's life and activities before 1892 are most elaborately catalogued in John R. Morris, "Davis Hanson Waite: The Ideology of a Western Populist" (Ph.D. Dissertation, University of Colorado, 1965).

6. Aspen *Union Era*, August 13, 1891.

7. *Ibid.*, November 19, 1891.

8. Undated address, Waite Papers, Colorado State Archives.

9. *Ibid.*

10. Aspen *Union Era*, January 7, 1892. Waite's commentary on land ownership was a paraphrase of a sentiment expressed by Thomas Jefferson in a letter to James Madison in 1789: "I set out on this ground, which I suppose to be self-evident, that the earth belongs in usufruct to the living; that the dead have neither powers nor rights over it." Jefferson to Madison, Paris, September 6, 1789. Paul L. Ford (ed.), *The Writings of Thomas Jefferson* (10 vols., New York, 1892-1899), V, 115.

11. *Ibid.*, June 23, 1892.

12. *Ibid.*, August 4, 1892.

13. Fuller, "Populist Regime in Colorado," 84.

14. These programmatic suggestions appeared frequently in the *Union Era*.

15. Undated address (probably 1892), Waite Papers.

16. Morris, "Davis Hanson Waite," 89.

17. Aspen *Union Era*, February 25, 1892.

18. *Ibid.*, August 13, 1891.

19. *Ibid.*, June 30, 1892.

20. *Colorado House Journal, Extra Session, 1894* (Denver, 1894), 46. The Latin reference is an ungrammatical rendition of *Cartago delenda est* ("Carthage must be destroyed"), a remark attributed to the Roman politician Cato (the Elder).

21. Waite, "A Phase of the Tariff Question," *Commonwealth*, III (June, 1890), 15-17.

22. Cited in Fuller, "Populist Regime in Colorado," 66.

23. *Ibid.*, 53.

24. *Ibid.*

25. Morris, "Davis Hanson Waite," 49-50; James E. Wright, *The Politics of Populism: Dissent in Colorado* (New Haven, 1974), a study of Colorado politics from 1876 to 1912, appeared after the manuscript of the present book was completed. Wright does not deal systematically with the character and philosophy of Davis Waite in his two chapters on Colorado's "Populist interlude," but he does demonstrate, by Pearson correlation coefficient computations, that Waite's electoral support came largely from miners, residents of mining towns (often foreign-born), and, to a lesser extent, from irrigation farmers. Waite knew nothing of correlation coefficients, but he was acutely aware of the sources of his political strength. But see Wright, *The Politics of Populism*, 153-155, 195-197.

26. *Ibid.*

27. *Colorado House Journal, 1893* (Denver, 1893), 109-126.

28. Harold F. Kountze, Jr., "Davis Hanson Waite and the People's Party in Colorado" (M.A. Thesis, Yale University, 1944), 29-30.

29. *Waite's Magazine*, I (October, 1898), 17.

30. The dismissals are detailed in Morris, "Davis Hanson Waite," 60.

31. C. L. King, *History of the Government of Denver* (Denver, 1911), 211.

32. Undated memorandum (1894), Davis H. Waite Papers, Colorado Collection, Denver Public Library.

33. *Waite's Magazine*, I (October, 1898), 1-26.

34. Fuller, "Populist Regime in Colorado," 90.

35. Morris, "Davis Hanson Waite," 217.

36. *Colorado House Journal, Extra Session, 1894* (Denver, 1894), 62.

37. *Ibid.*

38. This and the preceding quotation appear in the "Bloody Bridles" address. A manuscript copy of the speech is in the Colorado Historical Society, Denver, and the address was published in its entirety in 1894 by the Denver Trades and Labor Assembly as part of a *Souvenir of the AFL*. See also *Rocky Mountain News*, July 12, 1893.

39. Waite to Diaz, September 19, 1893; Diaz to Waite, January 11, 1894. Waite Papers, Colorado State Archives.

40. In 1877 the Republican-controlled legislatures of Ohio and Illinois adopted resolutions making silver coins, then demonetized by Congress, legal tender within their respective states. See Allen Weinstein, *Prelude to Populism: Origins of the Silver Issue, 1867-1878* (New Haven, 1970), 218.

41. Waite, "Are the Silver States Ruined?" *North American Review*, CLVIII (January, 1894), 24-29.

42. *Ibid.* and *Colorado House Journal, Extra Session 1894*, 52-62.

43. *Colorado House Journal, Extra Session, 1894*, 49-62, especially 49, 57.

44. *Boulder County Herald*, August 22, 1894.

45. *Colorado House Journal, 1895* (Denver, 1895), 64.

46. Waite to Robert Schilling, December 17, 1894. Waite Papers, Colorado State Archives. Schilling was a prominent Milwaukee labor figure and sometime Populist leader in Wisconsin.

47. Morris, "Davis Hanson Waite," 278ff.

48. *Waite's Magazine* appeared twice—October, 1898 and November, 1898.

49. *Waite's Magazine*, I (October, 1898), 31.

50. Denver *Times*, November 5, 1898. The reference was to James B. Weaver, the People's Party candidate for president in 1892, and to Marion Butler, Populist Senator from North Carolina and Chairman of the People's Party National Committee.

51. Waite to Henry Demarest Lloyd, June 13, 1897. Lloyd Papers, State Historical Society of Wisconsin.

52. Denver *Times*, November 5, 1898.

53. *Ibid.*, October 1, 1900.

54. The reference is to Hofstadter's essay in *The American Political Tradition and the Men Who Made It* (New York, 1948), 67-91.

55. *Waite's Magazine*, I (October, 1898), 31.

56. Morris, "Davis Hanson Waite," 245-250.

57. Undated address, Waite Papers, Colorado State Archives.

CHAPTER SIX: Populism in the State Legislatures: An Analysis of Seven Western States

1. The Omaha Platform may be most conveniently consulted in an Appendix to John D. Hicks, *The Populist Revolt* (Minneapolis, 1931), 439-444.

2. Walter T. K. Nugent, "Some Parameters of Populism," *Agricultural History*, XL (October, 1966), 255-270; O. Gene Clanton, *Kansas Populism: Ideas and Men* (Lawrence,

1969), 63-72, 198 *et passim*; see also Michael D. Boone, "The Washington State Legislature of 1897: A Study in Populism" (MA Thesis, Washington State University, 1966), 9-14.

3. This was especially true of Populism in Idaho, Kansas and Washington. Peter H. Argersinger's study, *Populism and Politics: William Alfred Peffer and the People's Party* (Lexington, 1974), appeared after the manuscript of the present work began its publishing sojourn. Argersinger postulated a dichotomy between the Populist movement and the People's Party and argued that the party, once it became penetrated by Democrats, corrupted the movement. See Argersinger, *Populism and Politics*, 36, 120, 127-128, 141-142, 160.

4. *Kansas House Journal, 1897* (Topeka, 1897); *Kansas Senate Journal, 1897* (Topeka, 1897). The exact figures were 924 House bills and 607 Senate bills.

5. *Kansas House Journal, 1897*, 46, 696; 46, 512; 539; 47, 296; 55, 224; 121, 454; *Kansas Senate Journal, 1897*, 71, 341.

6. *Kansas Senate Journal, 1897*, 186, 784-785; 63, 789; 40, 159; 45, 355; *Kansas House Journal, 1897*, 197, 648,; 90, 222, 331; 91, 294, 318, 48, 649.

7. *Kansas Senate Journal, 1897*, 63, 99, 789.

8. *Ibid.*, 498, 640-680; *Kansas House Journal, 1897*, 908.

9. See Clanton, *Kansas Populism: Ideas and Men*, 201-204.

10. *Kansas House Journal, 1897*, 908; *Kansas Senate Journal, 1897*, 679-680, 1091.

11. *Kansas House Journal, 1897*, 909. A railroad bill more satisfactory to the fusionist bloc was enacted in a special session called by Governor Leedy in December, 1898, but the new regulatory law was invalidated shortly thereafter in a Federal court case.

12. *Kansas House Journal, 1891* (Topeka, 1891); *Kansas Senate Journal, 1891* (Topeka, 1891).

13. *Kansas Senate Journal, 1891*, 120, 200, 774; 177, 480, 775; 97, 732, 836; 290, 476, 573; *Kansas House Journal, 1891*, 999; 789-790; 864, 747.

14. *Kansas House Journal, 1891*, 424, 713; 361, 624; 208, 27, 522-523; *Kansas Senate Journal, 1891*, 83, 372,; 805, 806-811.

15. *Kansas House Journal, 1891*, 16, 356; 208; 26, 266, 982; 27, 522-523; 361, 624; 424, 713; *Kansas Senate Journal, 1891*, 805, 806-811.

16. This conclusion is based upon an examination of the following: *Kansas House Journal, 1893* (Topeka, 1893); *Kansas Senate Journal, 1893* (Topeka, 1893); *Kansas House Journal, 1895* (Topeka, 1895); *Kansas Senate Journal, 1895* (Topeka, 1895).

17. *Nebraska House Journal, 1891, 1893, 1895, 1897, 1899* (York, Lincoln, 1891, 1893, 1895, 1897, 1899); *Nebraska Senate Journal, 1891, 1893, 1895, 1897, 1899* (York, Lincoln, 1891, 1893, 1895, 1897, 1899.

18. Stanley B. Parsons, "Who Were the Nebraska Populists?" *Nebraska History*, XLIV (June, 1963), 83-99.

19. David Stephens Trask, "Formation and Failure: The Populist Party in Seward County, 1890-1892," *Nebraska History* LI (Fall, 1970), 281-301, especially 289-290.

20. David F. Trask, "A Note on the Politics of Populism," *Nebraska History* XLVI (June, 1965), 157-161.

21. See Frederick C. Luebke, "Main Street and the Countryside: Patterns of Voting in Nebraska During the Populist Era," *Nebraska History* L (Fall, 1969), 260-263; see also Stanley B. Parsons, *The Populist Context* (Westport, Conn., 1973), 60-75, 121-141.

22. *Ibid.*, 266.

23. *Nebraska House Journal 1891, 1893, 1895, 1897; Nebraska Senate Journal, 1891, 1893, 1895, 1897.* Composition and party designations are indicated in the prefatory sections of each legislative journal.

24. *Nebraska House Journal, 1891* (York, 1891), 148, 149, 293, 356, 598, 509, 739, 904, 743; *Nebraska Senate Journal, 1891* (Omaha, 1891), 142. Page references here pertain only to the introduction of bills, not to their subsequent fate in the legislature.

25. *Nebraska House Journal, 1891,* 101, 188, 296, 678, 962, 189; *Nebraska Senate Journal, 1891,* 316, 368.

26. *Nebraska House Journal, 1891,* 966, 1648, 1875, 1882, 1899; 739, 1015; 293, 1004; 356, 1531; 508, 1078; 180, 422, 510, 624; 149, 625; 904, 1578-1579; 739, 1015; *Nebraska Senate Journal, 1891,* 142, 149.

27. *Nebraska House Journal, 1891,* 101, 496; 188, 1094; 307, 918; 295, 710; 962, 1539; 962, 1460; 188, 1268; 296, 1001, 455, 1023; *Nebraska Senate Journal, 1891,* 94, 1031; 316, 510; 358, 458, 474; 368, 740, 987, 1045.

28. *Nebraska House Journal, 1891,* 180, 422, 510, 624.

29. *Ibid.,* 966, 1648, 1875, 1882, 1899.

30. *Nebraska House Journal, 1893* (York, 1893), 323, 706-707, 313, 656, 890, 389, 675, 671, 568, 560; *Nebraska Senate Journal, 1893* (York, 1893), 83, 95, 249, 574, 419.

31. *Nebraska House Journal, 1893,* 323; 706-707; 313; 656; 389; 675; 671; 568; 560. *Nebraska Senate Journal, 1893,* 83, 501; 95, 333; 249, 406, 362, 574, 675-676; 419, 746.

32. *Nebraska House Journal, 1893,* 706-707; 656; 594; 650; 853; *Nebraska Senate Journal, 1893,* 83, 501. (The Nebraska railroad law was invalidated by the Supreme Court of the United States in March, 1898. *Smyth v. Ames* 169 U.S. 466.)

33; *Nebraska House Journal, 1895* (York, 1895), 190; 223; *Nebraska Senate Journal, 1895* (York, 1895), 117, 127.

34. *Nebraska House Journal, 1895,* 161, 1132, 1258, 1387.

35. *Nebraska House Journal, 1897* (Lincoln, 1897), 167; 173, 226, 493; 586; 263, 559; *Nebraska Senate Journal, 1897* (Lincoln, 1897), 120, 133, 134, 179, 329, 395, 369, 571, 808.

36. *Nebraska House Journal, 1897,* 188, 526, 993; 263, 721, 1015; *Nebraska Senate Journal, 1897,* 133, 452, 575.

37. *Nebraska House Journal, 1897,* 442, 992, 1148; *Nebraska Senate Journal, 1897,* 258, 582, 808; 369, 571, 808.

38. No negative votes were cast on the anti-trust bill and only two on the bill to extend the powers of the Board of Transportation. *Nebraska Senate Journal, 1897,* 571; 582.

39. *Nebraska Senate Journal, 1897,* 23, 26; *Nebraska Senate Journal, 1899* (Lincoln, 1900), 129; *Nebraska Senate Journal, 1901* (Lincoln, 1901), 92.

40. Kenneth E. Hendrickson, Jr., "Some Political Aspects of Populism in South Dakota," *North Dakota History,* XXXIV (Winter, 1967), 78, 86, 88-90; George M. Smith, *South Dakota and Its People* (Chicago, 1915), 675.

41. *South Dakota House Journal, 1897* (Pierre, 1897), 58, 319; 121, 181; 235, 1107; 235, 319; 325, 641, 642, 655; 678, 1050. See also Herbert S. Schell, *History of South Dakota* (2nd ed., Lincoln, 1968), 236-238.

42. *South Dakota Senate Journal, 1897* (Pierre, 1897), 52, 274, 449, 451; 207, 525, 835, 1044; *South Dakota House Journal, 1897,* 437, 972.

43. *South Dakota House Journal, 1897*, 713, 1275-1279, 1492; see also Burton Tiffany, "Initiative and Referendum in South Dakota," *South Dakota Historical Collections,* XII (1924), 331-333, 350.

44. *Ibid.,* 437; *South Dakota Senate Journal, 1897,* 274.

45. The internal struggles in the Lewelling and Leedy administrations (1893-1895; 1897-1899) in Kansas offered clear proof of the veracity of this contention, at least in the case of Kansas. See Clanton, *Kansas Populism: Ideas and Men,* 129-150, 185-229.

46. The best study of Idaho Populism is William J. Gaboury, "Dissension in the Rockies: A History of Idaho Populism" (Ph.D. Dissertation, University of Idaho, 1966).

47. Populists acquired power in Idaho, Montana and Washington only as a result of successful Populist-Democratic fusion.

48. The internal fragmentation in Colorado Populism is a recurrent theme in Leon Fuller, "The Populist Regime in Colorado" (Ph.D. Dissertation, University of Wisconsin, 1933); see also G. Michael McCarthy, "Colorado's Populist Leadership," *Colorado Magazine,* XLVIII (Winter, 1971), 31-34, 37-39.

49. *Colorado House Journal, 1893* (Denver, 1893), 176; 247, 1565; 319, 1567; 164, 414; 173, 1163, 1280, 1308; 175, 966; 175, 1736. *Colorado Senate Journal, 1893* (Denver, 1893), 402, 1396, 1478-1479, 1491.

50. *Colorado Senate Journal, 1893,* 242, 1492, 1730, 2196; *Colorado House Journal, 1893,* 1977; 181, 265; 32; 68, 71, 195.

51. *Colorado House Journal, Extra Session, 1894* (Denver, 1894), 110, 271; 114, 210-211; *Colorado Senate Journal, Extra Session, 1894* (Denver, 1894), 13-14.

52. *Idaho House Journal, 1893* (Boise, 1893), 28, 110, 97, 257; *Idaho House Journal, 1897* (Boise, 1897), 21, 103-104; 95, 125, 161-162; *Idaho Senate Journal, 1897* (Boise, 1897), 119, 142-143; see also William J. Gaboury, "From Statehouse to Bullpen; Idaho Populism and the Coeur d'Alene Troubles of the 1890s," *Pacific Northwest Quarterly,* LVIII (January, 1967), 16-19.

53. *Idaho House Journal, 1893; Idaho Senate Journal, 1893;* see also Claudius O. Johnson, "The Story of Silver Politics in Idaho, 1892-1902," *Pacific Northwest Quarterly,* XXXIII (June, 1943), 283-296.

54. *Idaho House Journal, 1895* (Boise, 1895), 10, 170; 23, 85, 165; 31; 70; 80; 82; 162, 235; 186, 232; *Idaho Senate Journal, 1895* (Boise, 1896), 60; 110, 141; 110, 152; 26-27; *Idaho House Journal, 1897* (Boise, 1897), 21, 93; 70; 78; 161, 208; *Idaho Senate Journal, 1897* (Boise 1897), 13, 67; 14, 70; 19, 82; 35, 147; 47, 92; 132.

55. *Idaho House Journal, 1897,* 98, 197; 21, 103-104; 21, 92; 95, 125, 161-162; *Idaho Senate Journal, 1895,* 119, 142-143; *Idaho House Journal, 1895,* 43; *Idaho House Journal, 1893,* 97, 257; 28, 110.

56. *Idaho Senate Journal, 1895,* 27.

57. *Idaho House Journal, 1895,* 31, 85, 165; 186, 232; *Idaho House Journal, 1897,* 98, 21, 93, 197; *Idaho Senate Journal, 1897,* 14, 70, 100.

58. See the discussion in Gaboury, "Dissension in the Rockies: A History of Idaho Populism," 220ff.

59. *Montana Senate Journal, 1897* (Helena, 1897), 26; 27; 64; 63; 101; 85-86; 102; 113, 26, 104; 17, 174, 179; 204-205, 227, 237; Thomas A. Clinch, *Urban Populism and Free Silver in Montana* (Missoula, 1970), 153-155.

60. The fullest studies of Washington Populism are: Michael D. Boone, "The Washington State Legislature of 1897: A Study in Populism" (MA Thesis, Washington State University, 1966); see also Carroll H. Woody, "Populism in Washington: A Study of the

Legislature of 1897," *Washington Historical Quarterly*, XXX (April, 1930), 103-119; and Fred R. Yoder, "The Farmers' Alliances in Washington—Prelude to Populism," *Research Studies of the State College of Washington*, XVI (September-December, 1948), 123-178.

61. *Washington Senate Journal* (Olympia, 1897), 75, 244, 570, 655; 600, 746; 69, 362; 103, 363; see also Boone, "The Washington State Legislature of 1897: A Study in Populism," 68ff; David B. Griffiths, "Populism in the Far West: 1890-1900" (Ph.D. Dissertation, University of Washington, 1967), 233.

62. *Washington Senate Journal, 1897*, 69, 616; 70, 611.

63. Boone, "The Washington State Legislature of 1897: A Study in Populism," 43-56; *Washington Senate Journal, 1897*, 409, 675, 680, 635-638, 722.

64. Boone, "The Washington State Legislature of 1897: A Study in Populism," 28-43.

65. *Ibid.*, 27.

66. *Ibid.*, 54-56.

67. *Ibid.*, 58-68; Thompson, "The Writings of John Rankin Rogers," 34-36, 55.

68. Boone, "The Washington State Legislature of 1897: A Study in Populism," 62-63.

69. This conclusion derives from examining the bills in the *Washington House Journal, 1897* and the *Washington Senate Journal, 1897*.

70. Gaboury, "Dissension in the Rockies," 76-78, 135-137 *et passim*; *Biennial Report of the Treasurer to the Governor of Idaho* (Boise; 1899). *Message of Governor Robert Burns Smith to the Fifth Legislative Assembly of the State of Montana* (Helena, 1897), 1-2.

71. Governor's Message, *Washington House Journal, 1899* (Olympia, 1899), 34.

72. Fuller, "The Populist Regime in Colorado," 90ff.

73. *Nebraska House Journal, 1891*, 148, 1181-1182.

74. Gabriel Kolko, *Railroads and Regulation, 1877-1916* (Princeton, 1965), 1-6, 7-29, 30-44, 64-83; see also A. B. Stickney, *The Railroad Problem* (St. Paul, 1891), for an example of an argument in favor of government regulation by a railroad executive.

CHAPTER SEVEN: The Futilitarians: Western Populists
in the House of Representatives, 1891-1900

1. *Congressional Directory*, 52 Cong., 1 Sess. (Washington, 1891), 43-47, 65, 73-74; 53 Cong., 1 Sess. (Washington, 1893), 325-331; 54 Cong., 1 Sess. (Washington, 1896), 364-370; 55 Cong., 3 Sess. (Washington, 1898), 307-313.

2. *Ibid.*

3. *Ibid.*, 53 Cong., 1 Sess., 325-331; 54 Cong., 1 Sess., 364-370.

4. *Ibid.*, 54 Cong., 1 Sess., 364-370.

5. *Ibid.*, 55 Cong., 3 Sess., 8-9, 19, 33-35, 65-66, 105, 126, 25, 51-52, 36, 81-83, 103, 3, 307-313.

6. *Ibid.*, 52 Cong., 1 Sess., 43-47, 65, 73-74; 53 Cong., 1 Sess., 23, 43, 44, 42, 62, 71-72; 54 Cong., 1 Sess., 17, 24, 97, 98, 82, 49, 364-370; 55 Cong., 3 Sess., 8-9, 18, 33-35, 65-66, 105, 126, 307-313; *Biographical Directory of the American Congress, 1774-1961* (Washington, 1961), *passim*.

7. The data are derived from election statistics in the biographical sections of *Congressional Directory*, 55 Cong., 3 Sess., 8-9, 18, 33-35, 65-66, 105, 126.

8. William Alexander Harris, for example, was criticized as "too fine haired and aristocratic." See Wynne P. Harrington, "The Populist Party in Kansas," *Collections of the Kansas State Historical Society*, XVI (1923-1925), 413, 443.

9. *Congressional Directory,* 52 Cong., 1 Sess., 43-44, 46-47, 65, 73-74; see also Hortense Marie Harrison, "The Populist Delegation in the Fifty-second Congress, 1891-1893" (MA Thesis, University of Kansas, 1933), 18-22.

10. New York *Times,* December 21, 1909; *Dictionary of American Biography* (22 vols., New York, 1932), VIII, 326-327; Kermit Opperman, "The Political Career of Senator William Alexander Harris" (MA Thesis, University of Kansas, 1938).

11. *Congressional Directory,* 53 Cong., 1 Sess., 23.

12. *Ibid.,* 52 Cong., 1 Sess., 43-44, 46-47, 65, 73-74; 53 Cong., 1 Sess., 23, 43, 42, 62, 44, 71-72; Harrison, "Populist Delegation in the Fifty-second Congress," 18-25.

13. *Congressional Directory,* 55 Cong., 3 Sess., 8-9, 18, 33-35, 65-66, 105, 126.

14. *Ibid.,* 3, 25, 51-52, 36, 81-83, 103.

15. *Congressional Directory,* 55 Cong., 3 Sess., 8-9, 18, 33-35, 65-66, 105, 126; *Biographical Directory of the American Congress, 1774-1961,* 516, 575, 673, 650, 710, 785. 972, 995, 1149, 1603, 1719, 1755 *et passim.*

16. See, for example, *Congressional Record,* 53 Cong., 2 Sess., 8398 (August 10, 1894); 55 Cong., 2 Sess., Appendix, 150-152 (January 31, 1898).

17. *Ibid.,* 55 Cong., 2 Sess., 764 (January 19, 1898). The name Rothschild appears with great frequency in Populist commentary in the House, and the famous English banking house served as a focal point for Populist animus toward financiers and as a symbol of contractionist and manipulative financial power. The other oblique references in the quotation are to J. Pierpont Morgan, the dominant figure in New York investment banking, and to Marcus Alonzo Hanna, Senator from Ohio, Chairman of the Republican National Committee and manager of William McKinley's presidential campaign in 1896.

18. See below, Populist analysis of war finance in 1898.

19. Expansion of gold coinage was a last resort, eliciting a favorable response from Populists in 1898 and 1899.

20. *Congressional Record,* 55 Cong., 2 Sess., Appendix, 549-551 (June 9, 1898); 55 Cong., 2 Sess., 4442 (April 29, 1898); 55 Cong., 2 Sess., Appendix, 746-749 (April 27, 1898); 55 Cong., 2 Sess., Appendix, 4410-4411 (April 28, 1898); 55 Cong., 2 Sess., Appendix, 430-437 (April 28, 1898); 55 Cong., 2 Sess., 4395-4400 (April 28, 1898); 55 Cong., 2 Sess., 4388-4390 (April 28, 1898); 55 Cong., 2 Sess., Appendix, 349-352 (April 28, 1898); 55 Cong., 2 Sess., 4408 (April 28, 1898); 55 Cong., 2 Sess., Appendix, 138-144 (January 31, 1898); 55 Cong., 2 Sess., 4400-4405 (April 28, 1898); 55 Cong., 2 Sess., 4324-4326 (April 27, 1898); 53 Cong., 3 Sess., 2195 (February 14, 1895); 52 Cong., 2 Sess., 612-617 (January 16, 1893). The above references comprise only a small sample.

21. *Ibid.,* 52 Cong., 1 Sess., 3009 (April 6, 1892); 53 Cong., 2 Sess., 8398 (August 10, 1894); 52 Cong., 1 Sess., 3008 (April 6, 1892); 52 Cong., 1 Sess., 6095 (July 12, 1892); 53 Cong., 1 Sess., Appendix, 542-545 (November 1, 1893).

22. *Ibid.,* 53 Cong., 2 Sess., 8398 (August 10, 1894), 2062 (February 9, 1894).

23. *Ibid.,* 52 Cong., 1 Sess., 128, 374, 461, 728, 1222, 1529, 2484; 53 Cong., 1 Sess., 773-776, 1003-1008, 3065, 3067; 53 Cong., 2 Sess., 3548, 3560, 2510-2524, 3460; 53 Cong., 3 Sess., 1866; 52 Cong., 1 Sess., 5774-5778, 5805-5807, 6132-6133, 1825-1832, 2495ff.; 53 Cong., 1 Sess., 242-243, 1003-1006; 55 Cong., 1 Sess., 1996, 721; 55 Cong., 2 Sess., 287, 1070, 826. This is a sample of the silver coinage bills introduced by twelve Populists, and, owing to their inconsequential nature, the dates of their introduction have not been included here. Dates for other Populist bills will also be deleted.

24. *Ibid.*, 52 Cong., 2 Sess., 1377-1383 (February 9, 1893); 54 Cong., 2 Sess., 2270-2277 (February 25, 1897); and various bills in 52 Cong., 1 Sess., 128, 374, 461, 1299, 1355, 1529.

25. *Ibid.*, 52 Cong., 1 Sess., 123, 289, 341, 378; 52 Cong., 2 Sess., 21, 190, 324; 55 Cong., 3 Sess., 2569, 52, 1013; 53 Cong., 2 Sess., 8395, 311.

26. *Ibid.*, 54 Cong., 1 Sess., 6292; 54 Cong., 2 Sess., 688-699, 180-181, dealing with reorganization and bonds of the Northern Pacific; see also 53 Cong., 2 Sess., 7603-7608; 52 Cong., 2 Sess., 1953-1958, 2241-2245; 55 Cong., 2 Sess., 2302, 879, 6720-6725, dealing with the debt of the Central Pacific.

27. But see *ibid.*, 53 Cong., 2 Sess., 1756, 6193, 7078-7080; and 52 Cong., 1 Sess., 976, 1120-1122, 1164, 2911-2916, 5071, 5077, 5081.

28. Retrenchment was a major Populist theme in the Fifty-fifth Congress.

29. Clanton, *Kansas Populism: Ideas and Men*, 274n.

30. *Congressional Record*, 52 Cong., 1 Sess., 3894 (May 3, 1892).

31. *Ibid.*, 53 Cong., 1 Sess., Appendix, 542-545 (November 1, 1893).

32. *Ibid.*, 52 Cong., 1 Sess., 2436-2437 (March 23, 1892); cf. Social Darwinist William Graham Sumner's observation that the acquisition of capital is "... the first requisite of every social gain, educational, ecclesiastical, political, aesthetic or other." William Graham Sumner, "The Challenge of Facts," in Albert G. Keller and Maurice R. Davie (eds.), *Essays of William Graham Sumner* (2 vols., New Haven, 1934), II, 97.

33. *Ibid.*, 53 Cong., 2 Sess., 1021 (January 18, 1894).

34. This was particularly true of Jerry Simpson, William McKeighan and William Baker.

35. *Congressional Record*, 53 Cong., 2 Sess., 1021, 1023 (January 18, 1894).

36. *Ibid.*, and 53 Cong., 2 Sess., Appendix, 105-107 (June 24, 1894); 55 Cong., 1 Sess., 143-147, 202-203, 206-209, 252, 271-273, 308-312, 336, 448, 535 (March 22, 23, 24, 25, 31, 1897); Appendix, 290-292, 358-362, 445-446 (July 11, 19, 1897).

37. *Ibid.*, 53 Cong., 2 Sess., 1060 (January 18, 1894).

38. *Ibid.*, 53 Cong., 2 Sess., Appendix, 105-107 (June 24, 1894); 55 Cong., 1 Sess., Appendix, 358-362 (July 19, 1897); 55 Cong., 1 Sess., Appendix, 260 (March 29, 1897).

39. *Ibid.*, 53 Cong., 2 Sess., 7195 (July 7, 1894); 53 Cong., 2 Sess., 1021-1023 (January 18, 1894).

40. See above, notes 35-39.

41. *Congressional Record*, 55 Cong., 1 Sess., 252, 308-312, 339-343, 336 (March 24, 25, 1897).

42. *Ibid.*, 252 (March 24, 1897).

43. See references in notes 35-42 and also 55 Cong., 1 Sess., Appendix, 201 (March 31, 1897); 55 Cong., 2 Sess., Appendix, 201, 690-695 (March 31, 1895; May 11, 1895); 55 Cong., 1 Sess., H.R. 3499, 1897; H.R. 10150, 4419.

44. *Ibid.*, 55 Cong., 1 Sess., Appendix, 260 (March 29, 1897).

45. This refrain appeared constantly in Populist commentary on the tariff, on silver and on federal bond policy.

46. *Congressional Record*, 55 Cong., 1 Sess., 274 (March 25, 1897).

47. Advocacy of treasury notes tended to replace silver in Populist monetary thought after 1896. See 55 Cong., 1 Sess., 721; 55 Cong., 2 Sess., 4289, 1123, 4178, 5059.

48. *Ibid.*, 52 Cong., 1 Sess., 6377.

49. *Ibid.,*53 Cong., 2 Sess., Appendix, 839-841 (June 5, 1894); 53 Cong., 2 Sess., 5794-5798 (June 9, 1894); 52 Cong., 1 Sess., 5081-5085 (June 6, 1892); 52 Cong., 1 Sess., 5077-5089 (June 6, 1892).

50. *Ibid.,* 53 Cong., 2 Sess., 5821 (June 5, 1894).

51. *Ibid.,* 53 Cong., 2 Sess., Appendix, 841 (June 5, 1894).

52. *Ibid.,* 55 Cong., 2 Sess., 561-566, 838 (January 12, 21, 1898); 55 Cong., 2 Sess., Appendix, 148-150 (January 21, 1898).

53. *Ibid.,* 55 Cong., 2 Sess., 828-836 (January 21, 1898); 55 Cong., 2 Sess., Appendix, 127-128 (January 31, 1898).

54. *Ibid.,* 53 Cong., 3 Sess., 2195 (February 14, 1895).

55. *Ibid.,* 55 Cong., 2 Sess., Appendix, 49-51 (June 9, 1898).

56. *Ibid.,* 55 Cong., 2 Sess., 4323-4324, 4388-4390, 4408, 4375, 4324-4326, 4442 (April 27, 28, 29, 1898); 55 Cong., 2 Sess., Appendix, 349-352, 746-749 (April 27, 28, 1898).

57. *Ibid.,* 55 Cong., 2 Sess., 4400-4405 (April 28, 1898).

58. *Ibid.,* 4379, 4440-4441, 4383-4384 (April 28, 29, 1898); Appendix, 138-144, 430-437 (January 31, 1898, April 28, 1898).

59. *Ibid.,* Appendix, 48-49 (January 31, 1898).

60. See above, notes 56, 57, 58, 59.

61. *Congressional Record,* 55 Cong., 2 Sess., Appendix, 359 (April 29, 1898).

62. *Ibid.,* 55 Cong., 2 Sess., 4384 (April 28, 1898).

63. *Ibid.,* 55 Cong., 2 Sess., 3745-3748 (April 12, 1898); Appendix, 279-281 (April 12, 1898); Appendix, 633-636 (June 14, 1898); Appendix, 304-306 (April 18, 1898).

64. *Ibid.,* 55 Cong., 2 Sess., Appendix, 304-306 (April 18, 1898); 764 (January 19, 1898); Appendix, 633-636 (June 14, 1898).

65. *Ibid.,* 55 Cong., 2 Sess., Appendix, 45-47 (January 20, 1898); even William McKinley was troubled by the prospect of uncontrolled American exploitation of the island. See Williams, *The Roots of the Modern American Empire,* 434-435, 525.

66. *Ibid.,* 55 Cong., 3 Sess., 1008-1012 (January 24, 1899); Appendix, 144-145 (February 24, 1899); 1055 (January 25, 1899).

67. *Ibid.,* 55 Cong., 2 Sess., 947-952 (January 24, 1898); 54 Cong., 1 Sess., 1624 (February 11, 1896).

68. *Ibid.,* 52 Cong., 1 Sess., 5740 (July 1, 1892); 6175-6179 (July 14, 1892); 53 Cong., 2 Sess., 7138-7139 (July 5, 1894).

69. *Ibid.,* 52 Cong., 1 Sess., 1077, 6010, 6015-6016 (February 11, July 11, 1892).

70. *Ibid.,* 55 Cong., 3 Sess., 1316 (January 31, 1899); Appendix, 90-94 (January 26, 1899); 1126-1128 (January 26, 1899).

71. *Ibid.,* 1001-1006 (January 24, 1899); 1264-1266 (January 30, 1899); Appendix, 90-94 (January 26, 1899).

72. *Ibid.,* 55 Cong., 2 Sess., 707-708 (January 17, 1898); 4503-4504 (May 2, 1898); 55 Cong., 3 Sess., 1264-1266 (January 30, 1899); 2329-2331 (February 24, 1899); Appendix, 229-230 (January 27, 1899).

73. *Ibid.,* 55 Cong., 3 Sess., Appendix, 229-230 (January 27, 1899).

74. *Ibid.,* and 1264-1266 (January 30, 1899).

75. *Ibid.,* Appendix, 90-94 (January 26, 1899).

76. *Ibid.,* 945 (January 23, 1899).

77. *Ibid.,* 52 Cong., 2 Sess., 412-415 (January 7, 1893); 55 Cong., 3 Sess., 1869-1870 (February 14, 1899); 55 Cong., 2 Sess., 6396 (June 27, 1898).

78. *Ibid.*, 55 Cong., 3 Sess., 87 (December 8, 1898).

79. *Ibid.*, 55 Cong., 2 Sess., 6396 (June 27, 1898).

80. *Ibid.*, 2974, 2979, 2992-2993, 3001, 3002-3003, 3011-3012 (March 18, 19, 1898).

81. *Ibid.*, 2991-2992, 3002-3003 (March 19, 1898).

82. *Ibid.*, reference in notes 80 and 81 above.

83. *Ibid.*, 3001 (March 19, 1898).

84. *Ibid.*, 2375-2378, 2442-2443 (March 2, 3, 1898); Appendix, 202-205, 258-260 (March 3, 1898).

85. *Ibid.*, 3011 (March 19, 1898).

86. *Ibid.*, 2991 (March 19, 1898).

87. *Ibid.*, 55 Cong., 3 Sess., 2593 (February 28, 1899).

88. *Ibid.*, 1401 (February 2, 1899).

89. *Ibid.*, 54 Cong., 1 Sess., 6292 (June 8, 1896); 54 Cong., 2 Sess., 688-689 (January 11, 1897); 53 Cong., 2 Sess., 7603-7608 (July 17, 1894); 53 Cong., 3 Sess. 1710-1711, 1763 (February 2, 4, 1895); 55 Cong., 2 Sess., 6720-6725 (July 6, 1898).

90. *Ibid.*, 55 Cong., 2 Sess., 879 (January 22, 1898).

91. *Ibid.*, 55 Cong., 1 Sess., 969, 982-985, 1007-1008 (May 10, 11, 1897).

92. *Ibid.*, 52 Cong., 1 Sess., 656 (January 28, 1892); 55 Cong., 2 Sess., 2680-2681, 2679-2680, 2706-2708, 2644-2651 (March 9, 10, 1898); Appendix, 49-51, 625-628 (March 10, 1898).

93. *Ibid.*, 55 Cong., 2 Sess., 2707 (March 10, 1898).

94. *Ibid.*, 54 Cong., 1 Sess., 5644-5646 (May 23, 1896); 53 Cong., 3 Sess., 3186-3190 (March 2, 1895); 53 Cong., 2 Sess., 8286-8287 (August 7, 1894).

95. *Ibid.*, 52 Cong., 2 Sess., 1559 (February 29, 1892).

96. *Ibid.*, 52 Cong., 2 Sess., 173-182 (December 15, 1892); 55 Cong., 1 Sess., 809 (April 22, 1897).

97. *Ibid.*, 54 Cong., 2 Sess., 1217-1235 (January 27, 1897); 1677 (February 9, 1897); 2946 (March 3, 1897); 53 Cong., 1 Sess., Appendix, 542-545 (November 1, 1893).

98. Clanton, *Kansas Populism: Ideas and Men*, 159, 167-168; Nugent, *The Tolerant Populists*, 156-157.

99. See, for example, Clanton, *Kansas Populism: Ideas and Men*, 274n.; *Congressional Record*, 52 Cong., 1 Sess., 3008, 6095 (April 6, July 12, 1892); 53 Cong., 2 Sess., 8395 (August 10, 1894). McKeighan observed that businessmen, "trained in the school of actual experience, know better how to conduct and regulate their own business than members of this or any other Congress know how to regulate it for them."

100. Kenneth Barkin, "A Case Study in Comparative History: Populism in Germany and America," in Herbert J. Bass (ed.), *The State of American History* (Chicago, 1970), 379.

101. G. Michael McCarthy found that Colorado's Populist leaders came from real estate, mercantile, legal and urban artisan backgrounds and continued to pursue these occupations after their brief involvement with reform. Few involved themselves in the Progressive movement. See McCarthy, "Colorado's Populist Leadership," *Colorado Magazine*, XLVIII (Winter, 1971), 30-42, especially 37-39, 41-42.

BIBLIOGRAPHY

Unpublished Sources

Allen, William Vincent. Papers, 2 Boxes. Nebraska Historical Society.

Boone, Michael D. "The Washington State Legislature of 1897: A Study in Populism" (MA Thesis, Washington State University, 1966).

Daniels, Dawn. "Lorenzo D. Lewelling—A Leader of the Kansas Populists" (MA Thesis, Northwestern University, 1931).

Flory, Raymond. "The Political Career of Chester I. Long." (Ph.D. Dissertation, University of Kansas, 1955).

Franks, Charles K. "Jerry Simpson—A Kansas Populist" (MA Thesis, Northwestern University, 1940).

Fuller, Leon W. "The Populist Regime in Colorado" (Ph.D. Dissertation, University of Wisconsin, 1933).

Gaboury, William J. "Dissension in the Rockies: A History of Idaho Populism" (Ph.D. Dissertation, University of Idaho, 1966).

Griffiths, David B. "Populism in the Far West: 1890-1900" (Ph.D. Dissertation, University of Washington, 1967).

Harrison, Hortense, Marie. "The Populist Delegation in the Fifty-second Congress, 1891-1893" (MA Thesis, University of Kansas, 1933).

Kountze, Harold F., Jr. "Davis H. Waite and the People's Party in Colorado" (MA Thesis, Yale University, 1944).

Lewelling, Lorenzo Dow. Papers. (Kansas Governor's Correspondence, Vols. 108-110). Kansas State Historical Society.

Lloyd, Henry Demarest. Papers. State Historical Society of Wisconsin, Madison.

Miller, Raymond Curtis. "The Populist Party in Kansas" (Ph.D. Dissertation, University of Chicago, 1928).

Morris, John R. "Davis Hanson Waite: The Ideology of a Western Populist" (Ph.D. Dissertation, University of Colorado, 1965).

Nebraska Farmers Alliance Papers. Nebraska Historical Society. 5 boxes.

Opperman, Kermit E. "The Political Career of William Alexander Harris" (MA Thesis, University of Kansas, 1938).

Scott, Mittie Y. "The Life and Political Career of William Vincent Allen" (MA Thesis, University of Nebraska, 1927).

Scott, Myron C. "A Congressman and His Constituents: Jerry Simpson and the Big Seventh" (MA Thesis, Fort Hays Kansas State College, 1959).

Thompson, Margaret Hollinshead. "The Writings of John Rankin Rogers" (MA Thesis, University of Washington, 1948).

Waite, Davis Hanson. Papers. Colorado State Archives, Denver.

Waite, Davis Hanson. Papers. Colorado Collection of the Western History Collection, Denver Public Library.

Waite, Davis Hanson. Untitled Address (The "Bloody Bridles" Address of July, 1893). MS Copy, Colorado Historical Society, Denver.

Walker, Samuel Emlen. "Populism and Industrialism: The Ideology of the Official Organ of the Nebraska Populist Movement" (MA Thesis, University of Nebraska, Omaha, 1970).

Government Documents

Biographical Directory of the American Congress, 1774-1961. Washington: G.P.O. 1961.

Colorado. *Journal of the House of Representatives, 1893; Journal of the House of Representatives, Extra Session, 1894; Journal of the Senate, 1893; Journal of the Senate, Extra Session, 1894.* Denver, 1893-1894.

Idaho. *Biennial Report of the Treasurer of the State to the Governor of Idaho.* Boise, 1899.

Idaho. *Journal of the House of Representatives, 1893, 1895, 1897; Journal of the Senate, 1893, 1895, 1897.* Boise, 1893-1897.

Iowa. *Iowa Documents, 1876. Reform School, Report of the Girls Department.* Des Moines, 1876.

Iowa. *Iowa Documents, 1880. Report of the Superintendent of the Girls Department of the State Reform School.* Des Moines, 1880.

Kansas. *Journal of the House of Representatives 1891, 1893, 1895, 1897; Journal of the Senate, 1891, 1893, 1895, 1897.* Topeka, 1891-1897.

Kansas. *Public Documents, 1893-1895.* Topeka: State Printer, 1895.

Kansas. *Kansas Public Documents, 1897-1898.* Topeka, 1898-1899.

Montana. *Journal of the House of Representatives, 1897; Journal of the Senate, 1897.* Helena, 1897.

Montana. *Message of Governor Robert Burns Smith to the Fifth Legislative Assembly of the State of Montana.* Helena, 1897.

Nebraska. *Journal of the House of Representatives, 1891, 1893, 1895, 1897, 1899; Journal of the Senate, 1891, 1893, 1895, 1897, 1899.* York and Lincoln, 1891-1899.

South Dakota. *Journal of the House of Representatives, 1897; Journal of the Senate, 1897.* Pierre, 1897.

United States, Congress. *Congressional Directory.* 52 Cong., 1 Sess.; 53 Cong., 1 Sess.; 54 Cong., 1 Sess.; 55 Cong., 3 Sess. Washington, 1891-1898.

United States, Congress, House of Representatives; United States, Congress, Senate. *Congressional Record.* 52 Cong., 1 Sess.; 52 Cong., 2 Sess.; 53 Cong., 1 Sess.; 53 Cong., 2 Sess.; 53 Cong., 3 Sess.; 54 Cong., 1 Sess.; 54 Cong., 2 Sess.; 55 Cong., 1 Sess.; 55 Cong., 2 Sess.; 55 Cong., 3 Sess. Washington, 1891-1899.

Washington. *Journal of the House of Representatives, 1895, 1897, 1899; Journal of the Senate, 1895, 1897, 1899.* Olympia, 1895-1899.

Newspapers

Alliance(Lincoln, Neb.), June 26, 1889.

Aspen (Colo.) *Union Era,* 1891-1892.

Barber County (Medicine Lodge, Kan.) *Democrat,* 1888.

Barber County (Medicine Lodge, Kan.) *Index,* 1886, 1888, 1889, 1893, 1897, 1898.

Boise *Idaho Daily Statesman*, 1894, 1899.
Boulder (Colo.), *County Herald*, August 22, 1894.
Denver (Colo.) *Times*, 1898, 1900.
El Dorado (Kan.) *Weekly Republican*, January 22, 1915.
Emporia (Kan.) *Gazette*, 1895, 1900.
Harper (Kan.) *Alliance Bulletin*, 1890.
Jerry Simpson's Bayonet (Wichita, Kan.), 1899-1900.
Kansas City (Mo.) *Star*, 1902, 1905.
Kansas City (Mo.) *Times*, December 16, 1930.
Manchester (N.H.) *Mirror and Farmer*, April 2, 1891.
Madison (Neb.) *Star*, July 31, 1896.
Medicine Lodge (Kan.) *Cresset*, 1888, 1897, 1898.
New York *Times*, December 21, 1909.
Omaha *Daily Bee*, Feb. 8, 1893.
Rocky Mountain News (Denver), July 12, 1893.
Topeka (Kan.) *Daily Capital*, January 10, 1893.
Topeka *Kansas Farmer*, October 8, 1890.
Topeka (Kan.) *State Journal*, 1893, 1900.
Wellington (Kan.) *People's Voice*, October 1, 1896.
Wichita (Kan.) *Daily Beacon*, September 5, 1890.
Wichita (Kan.) *Daily Eagle*, 1896, 1900, 1901, 1905.
Wichita (Kan.) *Sunday Eagle*, 1901.
Wichita *Kansas Commoner*, 1891, 1894.

Published Materials

Abramowitz, Jack. "The Negro in the Populist Movement," *Journal of Negro History*, XXXVIII (July, 1953), 257-289.

Allen, William Vincent. *Cuba Must Be Free*. Washington: G.P.O., 1898. (Reprint of Senate Address, 55 Cong., 2 Sess., 3410-3414 (March 31, 1898).

Allen, William Vincent. "Necessary and Natural Territorial Expansion," in William Jennings Bryan (ed.), *Republic or Empire: The Philippine Question*. Chicago: Independence Publishing Co., 1899. 287-304.

Allen, William Vincent. "The Necessity for the People's Party," *The Arena*, XXX (October, 1903), 410-414.

Allen, William V. *The Financial Policy*. Washington: G.P.O., 1896. (Reprint of Senate Address in *Congressional Record*, 54 Cong., 1 Sess., Appendix, 310-320 (April 30, 1896).

Allen, William Vincent. "Western Feeling Towards the East," *North American Review*, CLXII (May, 1896), 588-593.

Barkin, Kenneth. "A Case Study in Comparative History: Populism in Germany and America," in Herbert J. Bass (ed.), *The State of American History*. Chicago: Quadrangle, 1970. 373-404.

Barr, Elizabeth. "The Populist Uprising," in William E. Connelley (ed.), *A Standard History of Kansas and Kansans*. 5 vols. Chicago: Lewis Publishing Co., 1918, II, 1113-1195.

Bell, Daniel (ed.).. *The New American Right*. New York: Criterion Books, 1955.

Blankenship, Russell. "The Political Thought of John R. Rogers," *Pacific Northwest Quarterly*, XXXVII (January, 1946), 3-13.

Blodgett, Geoffrey. "Reform Thought and the Genteel Tradition," in H. Wayne Morgan (ed.), *The Gilded Age*. Rev. ed., Syracuse: Syracuse University Press, 1960. 55-76.

Chafe, William M. "The Negro and Populism: A Kansas Case Study," *Journal of Southern History*, XXXIV (August, 1968), 402-419.

Clanton, O. Gene. *Kansas Populism: Ideas and Men*. Lawrence: University of Kansas Press, 1969.

Clinch, Thomas A. *Urban Populism and Free Silver in Montana*. Missoula: University of Montana Press, 1970.

Coletta, Paolo E. "A Tempest in a Teapot? Governor Poynter's Appointment of William V. Allen to the United States Senate," *Nebraska History*, XXXVIII (July, 1957), 155-163.

Costigan, Walter J. "Lorenzo D. Lewelling," *Transactions of the Kansas State Historical Society*, VII (1901-1902), 121-126.

Diggs, Annie La Porte. *The Story of Jerry Simpson*. Wichita: Hobson Printing Co., 1908.

Farmer, Hallie. "The Economic Background of Frontier Populism," *Mississippi Valley Historical Review*, X (March, 1924), 407-427.

Ferkiss, Victor C. "Populist Influences on American Fascism," *Western Political Quarterly*, X (June, 1957), 350-373.

Fine, Sidney. *Laissez-faire and the General Welfare State: A Study of Conflict in American Thought 1865-1901*. Ann Arbor: University of Michigan Press, 1956.

Fite, Gilbert C. *The Farmers' Frontier, 1865-1900*. New York: Holt, Rinehart and Winston, 1966.

Ford, Paul L. (ed.). *The Writings of Thomas Jefferson*. 10 Vols. Washington: G.P. Putnam's Sons, 1892-1899. V.

Fuller, Leon W. "A Populist Newspaper of the Nineties." *Colorado Magazine*, IX (May, 1932), 81-87.

Gaboury, William J. "From Statehouse to Bullpen: Idaho Populism and the Coeur d'Alene Troubles of the 1890s," *Pacific Northwest Quarterly*, LVIII (January, 1967), 14-22.

Garland, Hamlin. "The Alliance Wedge in Congress," *The Arena*, V (March, 1892), 447-457.

Goodwyn, Lawrence C. "Populist Dreams and Negro Rights: East Texas as a Case Study," *American Historical Review*, LXXVI (December, 1971), 1435-1456.

Hackney, Sheldon. *Populism to Progressivism in Alabama*. Princeton: Princeton University Press, 1969.

Handlin, Oscar. "American Views of the Jews at the Opening of the Twentieth Century," *Publications of the American Jewish Historical Society*, XL (June, 1951), 323-344.

Harrington, Wynne P. "The Populist Party in Kansas," *Collections of the Kansas State Historical Society*, XVI (1923-1925), 403-450.

Haynes, Fred E. *James Baird Weaver*. Iowa City: State Historical Society of Iowa, 1919.

Hendrickson, Kenneth E., Jr. "Some Political Aspects of Populism in South Dakota," *North Dakota History*, XXXIV (Winter, 1967), 77-92.

Hicks, John D. *The Populist Revolt*. Minneapolis: University of Minnesota Press, 1931.

Hicks, John D. "The Sub-Treasury: A Forgotten Plan for the Relief of Agriculture," *Mississippi Valley Historical Review*, XV (December, 1928), 355-373.

Hofstadter, Richard. "John C. Calhoun: Marx of the Master Class," in Hofstadter, *The American Political Tradition and the Men Who Made It*. New York: Alfred A. Knopf, 1948. 67-91.

Hofstadter, Richard. *The Age of Reform: from Bryan to F.D.R.* New York: Alfred A. Knopf, 1955.

Holbo, Paul S. "Wheat or What: Populism and American Fascism," *Western Political Quarterly*, XIV (September, 1961), 727-736.

Jensen, Richard J. *The Winning of the Midwest! Social and Political Conflict, 1888-1896.* Chicago: University of Chicago Press, 1971.

Johnson Claudius O. "The Story of Silver Politics in Idaho," *Pacific Northwest Quarterly*, XXXIII (June, 1943), 283-296.

Johnson, Gerald W. *The Lunatic Fringe*. Philadelphia: Lippincott, 1957.

Kammen, Michael. *People of Paradox: An Inquiry Concerning the Origins of American Civilization.* New York: Alfred A. Knopf, 1972.

Keller, Albert G. and Maurice R. Davie (eds.). *Essays of William Graham Sumner.* 2 Vols. New Haven: Yale University Press, 1934. II.

King, Clyde L. *History of the Government of Denver.* Denver: Fisher Book and Stationery Co., 1911.

Kleppner, Paul. *The Cross of Culture: A Social Analysis of Midwestern Politics, 1850-1900.* New York: Free Press, 1970.

Kolko, Gabriel. *Railroads and Regulation, 1877-1916.* Princeton: Princeton University Press, 1965.

Leahy, David D. "Vagrant Memories of Fifty Years," El Dorado (Kan.) *Weekly Republican*, January 22, 1915.

Luebke, Frederick C. "Main Street and the Countryside: Patterns of Voting in Nebraska During the Populist Era," *Nebraska History*, L (Fall, 1969), 257-275.

Martin, Roscoe C. *The People's Party in Texas.* Austin: University of Texas Press, 1933.

McCarthy, G. Michael. "Colorado's Populist Leadership," *Colorado Magazine*, XLVIII (Winter, 1971), 30-42.

McDougal, Henry Clay. *Recollections, 1844-1909.* Kansas City, Mo.: privately printed, 1910.

McNeal, Thomas A. *When Kansas Was Young.* New York: Macmillan, 1922.

McSeveney, Samuel T. *The Politics of Depression: Political Behavior in the Northeast, 1893-1896.* New York: Oxford University Press, 1972.

Miller, Raymond Curtis. "The Background of Populism in Kansas," *Mississippi Valley Historical Review*, XI (March, 1925), 469-489.

Murdock, Victor. *Folks.* New York: Macmillan, 1921.

Nugent, Walter T.K. "Some Parameters of Populism," *Agricultural History*, XL (October, 1966), 255-270.

Nugent, Walter T.K. *The Tolerant Populists; Kansas Populism and Nativism.* Chicago: University of Chicago Press, 1963.

Parsons, Stanley B. *The Populist Context: Rural Versus Urban Power On A Great Plains Frontier.* Westport, Conn: Greenwood Press, Inc., 1973.

Parsons, Stanley B. "Who Were the Nebraska Populists?" *Nebraska History*, XLIV (June, 1963), 83-99.

Pollack, Norman. "Fear of Man: Populism, Authoritarianism, and the Historian," *Agricultural History*, XXXIX (April, 1965), 59-67.

Pollack, Norman (ed.). *The Populist Mind*. Indianapolis: Bobbs-Merrill, 1967.

Pollack, Norman. *The Populist Response to Industrial America: Midwestern Populist Thought*. Cambridge, Mass.: Harvard University Press, 1962.

Ridge, Martin. *Ignatius Donnelly: Portrait of a Politician*. Chicago: University of Chicago Press, 1962.

Ridgeway, Gordon B. "Populism in Washington," *Pacific Northwest Quarterly*, XXXIX (October, 1948), 284-311.

Rochester, Anna. *The Populist Movement in the United States*. New York: International Publishers, 1943.

Rogers, John Rankin. *Free Land; The Remedy for Involuntary Poverty, Social Unrest and the Woes of Labor*. Tacoma, Wash.: Tacoma Morning Union, 1897.

Rogers, John Rankin. *Homes for the Homeless*. Seattle: Allen Printing Company, 1895.

Rogers, John Rankin. *Life*. San Francisco: Whitaker and Ray, 1899.

Rogers, John Rankin. *The Inalienable Rights of Man*. Olympia, Wash.: the author, 1900.

Saloutos, Theodore. "The Professors and the Populists," *Agricultural History*, XL (October, 1966), 235-254.

Schell, Herbert S. *History of South Dakota*. 2nd ed., Lincoln: University of Nebraska Press, 1968.

Shaw, Albert. "William V. Allen: Populist," *Review of Reviews*, X (July, 1894), 30-42.

Sheldon, Addison E. "Nebraskans I Have Known: William Vincent Allen," *Nebraska History*, XIX (July, 1938), 191-206.

Simpson, Jerry. "The Knocker Who Knocks on the Knocker," *Kansas Knocker: A Journal for Cranks*, I (July, 1900), 19-20.

Simpson, Jerry. "The Plain People," *Illustrated American*, XXII (September 11, 1897), 332-334.

Simpson, Jerry. "The Political Rebellion in Kansas," in Nelson A. Dunning (ed.), *The Farmers Alliance History and Agricultural Digest*. Washington: Alliance Publishing Co., 1891. 280-283.

Smith, George M. *South Dakota and Its People*. Chicago: S.J. Clarke Publishing Co., 1915.

Sproat, John G. *The "Best Men"; Liberal Reformers in the Gilded Age*. New York: Oxford University Press, 1968.

Stickney, Alpheus B. *The Railroad Problem*. St. Paul: D.D. Merrill Co., 1891.

Thelen, David P. *The New Citizenship: Origins of Progressivism in Wisconsin, 1885-1900*. Columbia, Mo.: University of Missouri Press, 1972.

Tiffany, Burton. "Initiative and Referendum in South Dakota," *South Dakota Historical Collections*, XII (1924), 331-350.

Trask, David F. "A Note on the Politics of Populism," *Nebraska History*, XLVI (June, 1965), 157-161.

Vaile, Joel F. "Colorado's Experiment with Populism," *The Forum*, XVIII (February, 1895), 714-723.

Waite, Davis Hanson. "A Phase of the Tariff Question," *Commonwealth*, III (June, 1890), 12-18.

Waite, Davis Hanson. "Are the Silver States Ruined?" *North American Review*, CLVIII (January, 1894), 24-29.

Waite's Magazine, I (October-November, 1898).

Weinstein, Allen. *Prelude to Populism: Origins of the Silver Issue, 1867-1878*. New Haven: Yale University Press, 1970.

White, William Allen: *The Autobiography of William Allen White*. New York: Macmillan, 1946.

Wiebe, Robert H. *The Search for Order, 1877-1920*. New York: Hill and Wang, 1967.

Williams, William Appleman. *The Roots of the Modern American Empire*. New York: Random House, 1969.

Woodward, C. Vann. "The Populist Heritage and the Intellectual," *American Scholar*, XXIX (Winter, 1959-1960), 55-73.

Woody, Carroll H. "Populism in Washington: A Study of the Legislature of 1897," *Washington Historical Quarterly*, XXX (April, 1930), 103-119.

Yoder, Fred R. "The Farmers' Alliances in Washington—Prelude to Populism," *Research Studies of the State College of Washington*, XVI (September-December, 1948), 123-178.

INDEX

Allen, William Vincent: conservatism of, 43-44, 133n; career summarized, 44, 52; and sub-treasury, 44; and railroads, 44; and monetary policy, 44-47; and political reform, 45, 52; and People's Party, 45; and sectionalism, 49, 133n; and foreign policy, 50-51, 132n; mentioned, 18, 66, 68
    anti-monopoly theme (in Populism), 33-34, 44, 49, 67-68, 74, 113, 116
    Alliances, Farmers, 30, 44, 45, 56, 105
    Argersinger, Peter H., 142n

    Baker, William, 105, 109, 110, 116, 120, 147n
    Bell, John C., 18, 106, 110, 120
    Boen, Haldor, 110
    Botkin, Jeremiah, 122
    Bryan, William Jennings, 44, 74, 84
    Butler, Marion, 74, 141n

    Castle, Curtis H., 112, 118, 125, 126
    Cernuschi, Henri, 46, 47
    Clark, John Bates, 16
    Clover, Benjamin M., 40, 105, 110
    counterrevisionism: and Populist scholarship, 13-14, 131n

    Davis, John, 105
    debt (public): Populist attitudes toward, 37, 46-49, 58, 71, 114, 115, 116, 121, 122, 123. *See also* fiscal policy
    Diaz, Porfirio, 72
    Dingley tariff bill, 117, 118
    Donnelly, Ignatius, 40

    Ely, Richard T., 16, 128

    fiscal policy: Populist attitudes toward, 19-20, 22, 48, 58, 71, 91, 123-126; legislation concerning, 95-96. *See also* tariffs, debt, public spending, income tax